The Unfinished Puzzle

A 50-Day Journey To Strengthening Your Friendship with God

Ashley Alice White

Table of Contents

Acknowledgements

One of the most memorable gifts I ever received—material gifts, that is—was from my parents on one of my birthdays when I lived in Massachusetts. I was probably turning about eight or nine years old that year and I got a special desk I had been waiting and longing for.

I was so excited to use it because I could do my homework on it, play office and teacher with my sister, and put all my new pencils, papers, and erasers in it. I still remember the feeling I had when I saw that desk in my living room. More importantly, I was so happy it was mine.

Gifts we receive from people, such as friends and family, co-workers, and sometimes strangers, can be quite special. Depending on what that gift is, it can remain with us forever. These gifts can be material gifts or gifts such as an exchange of kind words, the knowledge of something, or a talent.

As I experienced joy from material gifts before, such as the desk on my birthday, I have also received a gift that was not materialistic, and I could never replace it. That desk that made me so happy as a child was replaceable.

This gift I now have will never go out of style. There will never be a better version, and no one can steal it from me. It has become a part of me that will never leave. It is not replaceable.

It's knowledge.

I was shown and instructed on who God is by my parents. They incorporated the Lord's love into my mind but also let me choose. I was able to receive a beautiful and irreplaceable gift of knowledge about who the Lord is, and it saved my life. It gave me hope. I learned wisdom and was able to apply it to my life wherever I was in the world.

I cherish this gift always because my life was saved the moment I met God. They gave me knowledge of Him and it saved my life which I find to be the greatest thing I'll ever receive in my lifetime.

To my Father and my Mother,

I thank you for giving me the chance to know God, for now I am able to share and encourage others with the hope the Lord has given me. The knowledge and wisdom you chose to give me is incomparable to anything I have ever received. Your support is overwhelmingly appreciated. Your love is like no other. Your selflessness is like a light from above. I am forever indebted to you both. So much love from my heart to you.

Friends,

You know who you are, and I think the world of you. You all have supported me endlessly, and the word thank you will never show how grateful I am for every single one of you. The smile you give me from day to day is remarkable.

I thank everyone who picks up this book. For my intent for each of you who reads this is to come along this ride with me and leave encouraged and hopeful after reading each word.

More importantly, I hope that you feel the everlasting love from God and know that you are forgiven. You are enough, you are loved, and that there is a way out of the long dark tunnel you might be in. Please know and believe that there is hope always, and there is real love. You just need to find it and find the Author of it who happens to also be the Creator of the universe.

Xo

Introduction

Puzzles can be so difficult. In fact, I admire the patience of anyone who enjoys them. It is especially difficult when it's a big picture with many details involved.

Also, when there are all sorts of different colors and lines, you tend to get confused on where each piece fits. It gets frustrating, and most people quit.

I've definitely quit before. Actually, I always quit. Now that I'm thinking about it, it's even worse when you of course pick up the piece that goes right smack down in the middle of the puzzle. You have no clue where to align the other pieces or even begin because it doesn't look familiar yet.

Think of your life as an unfinished puzzle where you only see certain pieces. Some are scattered, and some don't fit in certain areas. It's frustrating to us because we can't see the whole picture yet. Sometimes we just see a glimpse, and other times it looks like nothing at all. It's natural for us to get frustrated when we can't see. This makes us often not know where to begin.

God made these puzzles. He made every single one. He created them so uniquely, so distinctly, and made them all so special that only He can see the whole picture.

This unfinished puzzle is your life. We keep trying to force pieces to fit with each other because we can't see the big picture and we get impatient. We end up just trying to put them anywhere because we want to move on to the next thing.

As we try so hard to force things to happen in our life, especially when we know it's not the right thing, and know very well it won't last, these puzzle pieces in our life over time become damaged. Just like puzzles we try to do, forcing the pieces to stay together when it's not the right fit, just won't work. It will never become a picture.

Trust God with your puzzle. He sees the whole picture and knows where everything goes. After all, He created it.

You may be going through something today and don't understand it at all. You could be devastated and want to know why God would allow something like this happen to you. I get it, because I do that at times.

Are you sick and not sure how you will ever get better? Maybe you can't pay for your house anymore, or your spouse left you.

It's tough to think in the moment of these trials we go through, that God's got it and that His hands are in this very situation. It's hard to know he sees the entire picture, especially when you feel like you're drowning.

I get it.

But please know He has your very next step set out for you. It's perfectly planned. We don't know what could happen tomorrow, in seconds, or in years from now, which is terrifying.

Trust in God. Know He sees the whole picture, and He will not waste your pain.

Let His perfect hands finish your puzzle.

So, my advice is to surrender your puzzle. When you stop forcing things to happen or fit together, like we

sometimes do with puzzles when we can't figure them out, you can give it up to God. Surrender. God's plans He made for you before you were born will unfold, and you will come to see they are far beyond what you have ever dreamed.

I intend for you to be hopeful and encouraged, and I believe that you can surrender. Whether you read just this page, or read the entire book, I hope you fight for your joy and peace God can deliver to you.

So cheers to you my friend, and welcome aboard this journey of surrendering your puzzle where you meet your final destination: Hope.

Please prepare for your gate departure. This is a non-stop flight departing from fear, doubt, anxiety, anger, and sadness traveling to your final destination: Hope. You will experience peace, joy, everlasting love, and forgiveness from our Captain who is our Lord and Savior, Jesus Christ.

Fasten your seat belt. This is the journey of your life.

Foreword by Ashley Emma

Life is a puzzle.

This is just one of the many original analogies I've never heard of or even thought of until I read *The Unfinished Puzzle* by Ashley Alice White.

Ashley truly is wise beyond her 22 years. She sees things differently. As I read this book, I was amazed at how she made things make sense by using real life examples that made the concepts easy to understand. I kept thinking, *I've never thought of it that way.*

As I read this, I felt as though a good friend was chatting with me over tea, gently showing me the refreshing truth.

This devotional is raw and eye-opening. It will make you look at life and your relationship with God differently.

Many of us Christians were raised in the church, going to Sunday school or youth group, learning about God. Or maybe you didn't find God until you were older and you learned about Him then. Either way, we spend time learning about God, which is definitely a good thing, but is it enough?

We may know a lot *about* God, but do we actually *know Him?*

Have you ever heard the song "Jesus is a Friend of Mine?"

The Lord wants to be your friend.

Maybe you see God as a distant ruler domineering over the

universe, or as an absent or strict father.

Do you see Him as a friend? Someone you can get close to and can't wait to spend time with? Someone you can easily talk to and share your struggles, successes, and joys with?

This book will change the way you see God.

Maybe you feel like a fraud and that you shouldn't pray, or that you can't possibly be forgiven. Maybe you feel like you need to clean up your messy life before you invite Him in.

As Ashley says, God sees all your messes. He loves you no matter what. You don't need to pretend like you have it all together before talking with Him.

Realize God can be your best friend, and a friendship is a two-way relationship. When you pray to Him, you must also listen to His response.

Yes, God rules the universe and made everything in existence, but He still wants your heart. He wants you to open up to Him and tell him about your bad day or about what you're excited about. He cares about every detail of your life.

So invite Him into your life today, messes and all, and become His friend.

And as you read this book, open up your mind to the possibilities. Over these next 50 days, if you stick with it, you will become closer to God and get to know Him better personally.

Let Him and this book change your life.

-Ashley Emma, bestselling author of Undercover Amish

Day 1: Take off

This four-letter word brings light to the world. If it were a color, it would be the most delicate pastel. It brings happiness to your eyes as you glow when you have it. It's the light at the end of the tunnel. It is within you and the very last thing you have to hold onto.

However, if we do not have it from God, it won't be the real thing. I think you are starting to get closer to knowing what this word is, so I will give you a few more clues. It is something you naturally do every day. You look forward to it. You dream with it. Some people embody it.

Hope.

Hope is a special gift from God that only He can deliver. It is important to know that we will never run out of it. It is our lifeline.

Since we'll always have this desirable feeling to look forward too, we must never forget it and always believe it. God intended us to not only hope, but to hope passionately. We cannot undermine God's work by rarely hoping or having small hopes and small prayers.

He is a big God and waits for your biggest requests and your biggest dreams within his will of course. He gave you hope, so go ahead—hope. Hope passionately. Hope for the love of your life, hope for happiness and peace, and hope for a better and bigger future.

We cannot let fear interrupt our hopes and prayers because the Creator of the universe is a lot bigger than fear. Do not allow anymore interruptions.

We don't need to fear interruptions because what comes from God cannot be denied. What the Lord gives you, nothing and no one shall take it away. What He says is yours will be yours.

God is in control at all times. He calms all storms.

When you think that there is no hope, like there is absolutely nothing left, remember the truth I told you. Remember that the Lord, our merciful God, has the power to make anything He wants happen, however he won't do anything contrary to his will and purpose.

When you feel there is no hope, remember that your entire situation can be turned around in the matter of a moment.

God has the world right in the palm of His hand. If you have a moment, look at your hand right now, try and fit something relatively small between your thumb and pinky finger. It's pretty small if it fits there, right?

That is how God feels holding the universe. It's easy to forget how big He is and how much control He has because we can't see Him. But when we walk by faith and not by sight, our hope and strength become stronger. When we walk by faith, we are able to hope and trust in His plan. His desire is to give us what our heart longs for, which is why we need to hope in Him and pray for what we desire.

Do not just hope, but hope passionately. When you hope and pray to God, is it passionately, or are you just asking for small things you will settle for?

Don't be cliché with God. He created you and he knows

you. He designed your heart. Think of the riskiest idea, feeling, or thing you hope for, and pray hard. Ask him for it. Dwell in His presence. Make your passion to find hope every day in each situation you are in, even when someone tells you it is impossible.

This small word is what keeps us going, because without hope what would we have when things significantly drop? We wouldn't survive. Do not leave this precious gift unwrapped and forgotten. Treat it like the most extraordinary powerful force, because that's how it is when God gives it to you. This thing we call hope radiates light in the darkest of times.

So go ahead, hope. Passionately hope.

Day 2: Nice to Meet You Again, Rock Bottom

I thought when I met you, it would be our last encounter. That this was it, there wouldn't be another time. This was our final meeting, I repeatedly played over and over again in my mind. Going up is the only direction I can go from here. It was almost like you brought a little dose of hope, because us meeting would only mean things would get better. There was nothing lower. But I was wrong, we met again.

Nice to see you again, rock bottom.

Time after time we may think: *This is it, I've reached the bottom.*

You descend and hit the floor. It's the most painful, hopeless thing life has to offer. It's twisted because it gives a tiny glimpse of hope—from there we can only go up. Then that lovely encounter you had with rock bottom comes swiftly by with something new, sometimes again and again.

What do we do when we get there? We can't change the fact that bad things happen to us and that we may hit "rock bottom" while it abandons us with the feeling of utter emptiness.

I have a question for you. What if we changed the way we welcomed rock bottom when it unexpectedly visits?

I know that sounds bizarre and probably sounds like I've never endured the actual real pain that rock bottom so handsomely delivers to us. But I have, believe me I know the lowest a person can go; I've been on the floor.

I've felt the gut wrenching sadness, and I've dealt with the overbearing, debilitating anxiety that is attached to it.

But if you would just try and greet rock bottom when it visits, in a different manner than you have before, you'll notice a difference. Do not be hopeless this time around, welcome your guest in a new manner. Show hospitality.

Be hopeful because you have God on your side, which means you won't drown—instead, you will breathe. Greet this dreadful thing with hope and ambition to fight for your joy.

When you have hope in God, you cannot lose, and you cannot drown. Be hopeful that the Lord is with you during these times where He can use your troubles for good. He will pull you out of the water you are in when your visitor arrives and use your pain for victorious measures you can't begin to fathom.

The times you hit the floor will be for a reason, whether you're learning, growing, or discovering God's purpose for you.

Get to know the rock bottom you hit and the emotions that accompany it. Enjoy a cup of coffee with it! Stay a while. For the second time around, you'll know how to better manage yourself and the rollercoaster of emotions that comes with it.

As Psalm 119:50 says, "My comfort in my suffering is this: Your promise preserves my life."

Think of all the promises from God right now and keep them in mind. Have hope during these times of trial, because your new perspective on the encounters you have with rock bottom will be much different and easier as the Lord promises to hold your hand. When you welcome this unfortunate visitor with a positive mindset, as well as hope and grace, you will see the Lord's purpose for you.

Even when you hit rock bottom, you have many promises from God, and you'll still get out of the water. The Lord knows exactly how much you can handle, and He knows why you've hit the floor. Feel comforted, today, because the Lord goes with you and he will comfort you when you're at your lowest.

Greet rock bottom. Welcome it. Address it with the promises from God and hang in there. You have a life filled with hope, a strong powerful hope. Know, always, that the Lord holds your hand. Look up to Him during these times.

Day 3: New Day, New Creation

It's so devastating when natural disasters happen and wipe out entire villages, cities, and towns, leaving places demolished and even taking many lives much of the time. Although I have never had to endure that type of devastation, I do feel for the people who have.

As I was in Haiti with my father, I remember when he spoke to the village of Pavillon about opportunities.

He said, **"God created each day, and each day is a new day God can create a new opportunity."**

I remember everyone cheering and clapping because it gave them hope and they believed, like us, that there is always hope, even in their circumstances such as after effects of hurricanes.

Since there have been many times their villages have been ruined due to natural disasters, it leaves them with nothing. They have to start all over again which makes many of them feel hopeless.

This was a precious time as well as an eye-opening time for me because these people who don't have much still work hard and hope every day. **Although you and I may not be experiencing a natural disaster at this very moment where our house or neighborhood has been wiped out, I am sure there are aspects in your life that have been wiped out and feel like a disaster where you have to start all over again.**

With anything that is happening in your life right now or has happened, there is hope.

You may think there is nothing left for you or that your circumstance will never get better. Maybe you've accepted that there's nothing else you can do, so you settle and move on.

So many negative thoughts might spill into your mind. You might think you will never have a better marriage, get a better job, or have a child.

You're partially right because you can't do those things on your own, but you can with God. Each day he can create a beautiful marriage, bless you with a child, and open a door to a new job.

Each day is a new opportunity for a new creation. Many of the words throughout the Bible, especially in the very beginning, say "God created."

Pray to God and ask Him for a new creation. Something might be broken in your life, but the Lord can create something from that.

When you pray continually, passionately, and look for the will of God, you will see a new creation. Have hope today that any area of your life may become a new creation. While you wait, ask the Lord for strength with patience, as it is always His timing.

Genesis 1:1 says, "In the beginning God created the heavens and the earth."

He created then, He creates now, and He will create.

Day 4: Who Do You Pick for Your Team?

Thinking back to when I was in elementary school, middle school, and even high school, we would play different games that involved us picking teammates and partners.

Sometimes we picked our teammates, and sometimes the coach or teacher did. Either way, I would always have a pretty good idea of who I wanted on my team. It's natural to have an idea.

I had a few friends that were exceptionally talented at soccer, so when we played, I knew I wanted them on my team, as we would most likely win all together.

Even when you are in school working on projects, sometimes you have to pick a partner for that too. Obviously, you are going to pick someone you think would be a good choice because you want to do your best and get a great grade, or in some people's cases pick someone who will do all the work.

Maybe even at work there are projects where teams are put together to work on special projects, you will want to have an exceptional team so you do well, which goes to show it doesn't matter the age you are you will always have to pick people to work with. There are so many different times in life where we have to work with others and choose who is on our team.

In life, we choose people to be on our team that we think of in high regards, so we have the best support.

So whose team do you want to be on? God's or the world's? The world will fail you, so you won't do as well, but God will never fail you and you will always win with Him.

I had to ask myself this question a long time ago and continue to do so while making decisions every day.

Daily, we need to pick who is on our team, or whose team we are on. So here is your time to choose. Is it God, or is it the world? Do you want to win in this challenging, yet amazing, thing called life with God, or be on your own with the world?

When thinking of problems you have, don't think that you have a big problem. Instead know and believe you have a big God. He is bigger than anything you have to face. The world will never be there for you the way He is. He is the ultimate teammate, as He is worthy, reliable, dependable, and omniscient. Pick God as your teammate, you'll never be alone.

Deuteronomy 20:4 says, "For the Lord your God is the one who goes with you to fight for you against your enemies to give you victory."

God wants you to be victorious. He wants you to prosper and win. He knows you can't do it alone which is why He wants to be with you. He will never leave you.

Choose God in this game of life.

Day 5: You've Got a Friend in Me

Most of you probably know the movie *Toy Story*. It was one of my childhood favorites as I always watched it with my siblings. Do you remember when the song "You've Got a Friend in Me" sung by Randy Newman, came on? I'm not exactly sure when it exactly plays or the scene, and I'm not even sure of all the words, but I know exactly what song it is right when the music starts.

That song was somehow stuck in my head while I was in Haiti. I'm not sure how it even got into my head because I don't remember anyone bringing it up, and it certainly was not playing.

It was during a time when I was feeling alone which made me miss my friends back home a little, at first. Even though I was with my Dad, and I was with other people we had met in Haiti, I still felt lonely because I wasn't familiar with my surroundings or many people who were there. As I thought about it and kept humming the tune a little bit, I was reminded how I have a friend in God. He wanted me to lean on Him and know that I was not alone.

There was barely electricity where we stayed, which was considered to be somewhat better than most parts of the country as many people didn't have electricity. I felt even more alone because I couldn't just call or text one of my friends to tell them what I had been doing and what I had seen. This was a true test to my relationship with the Lord, because I didn't know what to do when I was wide awake not being in my usual surroundings. I had a book with me and a journal, so I could entertain myself with those two things, but the test I'm talking about was who I would turn to in those times.

I used that time to turn to God as my friend and talk to Him. To lean on Him. I shared with Him how I was feeling and that I really needed His strength during this time.

In life, our friends and family will be there for us a lot of the time, but it is physically impossible for them always to be. When we are wide awake at 3:00am, we can't just go wake them up and ask to talk or ask for strength. But we can do that with God. He's always there.

As I did this, I felt better because I knew when I have no one to turn to, and when I'm in a strange country where I can't speak their language, I have God.

Since I live in the United States, where the majority of my friends and all of my family live, it is easy for me to communicate with them and be around them, so it's not so rough when I feel alone and hopeless.

Because I was in Haiti and I couldn't communicate with them at all, even though my father was there, and I could have talked to him, there were times we weren't together. I had to turn to God. I experienced for the first time that wherever we are, He is.

This was a time my faith really expanded, and I started to know God as a friend. I had that song stuck in my head, and I am so glad I did because I was able to look at God as a forever and always friend.

As you read this, I hope you are encouraged, wherever you are, whatever you are doing, and know that you always have a friend in God. Even if you feel alone and like He is not listening, He is. He is there.

God doesn't leave you, even in the scariest situations where you feel He abandoned you, He pulls through.

He is your friend who never gives up. Remember the song played in *Toy Story*, even if it's silly, because you do have hope when times are trying and you are scared, or you just feel lonely, even if you are with people. **The Lord tells us, "You've got a friend in me."**

John 15:13 says, "Greater love has no one than this: to lay down one's life for one's friends."

You may think your best friend is the greatest and that there is no other like him or her. I think that about my best friend too, but I also know she is incapable of always being there for me, because she's human. I know she will make mistakes because of that.

Think of God as your best friend who died for you, because he did as well as go through pain, anguish and discomfort before the cross just for us. Which of your friends would lay down their life for you? Most likely not all your friends would do that without hesitation.

Know that the Lord is always your friend and is there for you at all times. Have hope during your loneliest times.

Day 6: The Purpose of Pain

It was two days after my birthday, though I can't remember which birthday it was, maybe my 12th or 13th. That was when my best friend's mother passed away. I didn't know what it was like to lose a parent, so it was hard for me to say anything to her besides, "I am here for you, and I am so sorry."

Since I didn't know what it was like and didn't understand her level of pain, I couldn't tell her I understood. I didn't know how to identify with her pain because I hadn't endured it before.

When we go through pain, we don't always know the reason for it. We become angry, upset, and confused when we're hit with it.

I become significantly discouraged when dealing with emotional pain. It's one of my many flaws. Sometimes it's actually scary to be around us, for our friends and family anyway, because we become a different person when we are in pain. Sometimes we become depressed, mean, mad, and discouraged. It's like a tornado of emotions that shows up for a bit to take over. It's unfair. I know that, and the Lord does too. He knows how it feels to endure pain, so we are never alone, for He felt it first.

Imagine if we never went through pain. Your immediate answer would be that it would be amazing.

Imagine no pain at all, on this earth. Would we ever learn, or we would just stay the same and become dull and possibly ignorant?

For example, when you are a kid and you ride your bike without a helmet and fall and hit your head, obviously you are in pain. You learn to always wear your helmet from then on. What did you get from that?

Growth.

There are purposes for your pain: learning, growing, and developing. You may not understand it, and obviously not like it, but there is a purpose. It's to teach you.

This pain is your teacher. Let it teach you but not debilitate you.

Back to what was said in the beginning about understanding pain. I couldn't identify with my best friend's pain when her mother passed away from cancer, because I had not gone through that sort of pain and suffering before. I didn't know the true gut wrenching feeling she was experiencing.

I am sure she felt angry and hurt and had all sorts of open wounds, but I just couldn't identify with those exact feelings.

Really focus on this next part.

The Lord can identify with our pain, always. Re-read that last word. Always. He always knows how we feel, every ounce of pain and sting from our open wounds. He identifies with us. Remember that he suffered on the cross for us and literally died a horrible, brutal death so we wouldn't have to.

He knows horrible pain—He endured it first before you and I. He knows how it feels to be misunderstood and isolated because He was slandered. He knows! He was nailed to a cross, He was mocked, and He was shamed. He can identify with all of our pain. He has had friends turn on him.

Think about how many people deny Him and slander Him every day.

When you are in pain, with open wounds, wondering why you feel this way and how to stop it, know that the Lord will not waste your pain.

There is a reason for it and during the process you will develop. Not only that but you have someone by your side that understands and identifies with you. You are always understood by the God of this universe because everything you went through and are going through right now, He went through first.

When your friends don't know how you feel and can't empathize with you, the Lord can, so turn to Him.

Pain is your teacher. Draw close to God, especially during your most painful times, because He knows how you feel and knows the purpose of it. You may not understand it now, but you don't have too. The Lord will come through, and He will give you His strength.

Psalm 91:1 says, "Whoever dwells in the shelter of the Most High will rest in the shadow of the Almighty."

When you draw near to God and dwell in His shelter, you will be comforted. You can rest in His shadow.

When you are in pain, lean on the Lord. His peace will overwhelmingly comfort you.

You are probably thinking it's easy for me to say this because I do not know anything that you are going through right now, and that there is no hope for your situation. Well, you are slightly correct.

I said slightly because you are right about the fact that I don't know anything you are going through. Maybe right now what you are going through I may not even have the knowledge of its existence, but that doesn't matter because the Lord does. The Lord knows everything you are going through because He went through it and felt it.

You heard that, right? He has felt that way you are feeling now.

As I say these hopeful things, it might sound easy and like it's coming from someone who hasn't had it hard. Maybe you're right. Compared to many people, I don't have to struggle, but there is always a struggle with each person, and you would be surprised about what people you know go through.

It was never easy for me to believe and have faith in any of this because I'm human.

I have not only heard, but actually experienced the hope and comfort God brings in unbearable times. Dealing with anxiety and overwhelming sadness is something I have struggled with resulting from all sorts of hardships like illnesses which I believe to be my hardest one thus far. However, having faith and hope is the one thing that got me through it because I know I had one person to count on that would never forsake me: God. I believed He had a bigger plan and trusted that He would get me through it all which was when I felt His comfort. I know how it is, and I want you to dwell in His presence too, for you will have much peace and joy.

Lean on God not only through times of pain and adversity, but through happy times and blessed times. Always draw near to Him, for He will always be there to comfort and sustain you.

The Lord will not waste your pain; He always has a purpose. **When you don't see the purpose yet, you will learn and strengthen your faith in the meantime.**

The Lord will make what you are going through of great purpose for He has plans to prosper you, not to harm you. Trust Him.

Romans 8:18 "I consider that our present sufferings are not worth comparing with the glory that will be revealed in us."

You may be in a lot of pain now, but it will not be compared to the joy the Lord will bring you. Your blessings will be doubled for the pain you endure. Keep learning from this pain and drawing near to God.

Day 7: Wait for Your Reward

I went to a fundraiser where Bob and Pam Tebow spoke. They are missionaries with five children, one of them being the well-known Tim Tebow, who show great example of amazing faith in the Lord. I heard a short story that I hope to never forget. I remember hearing it and wanting to write it down, so I would remember it later on. I repeated it in my head so many times, over and over again to instill it in my mind which worked because now I have the opportunity to share it with you.

I don't know it word for word, but I do remember the gist of it which brought me a lot of encouragement.

That night, Pam Tebow told a story about how her son, Tim, where they both went to an award show together, however she didn't mention what it was for or why they were there, unless I missed that part. At that award show, he had looked at her and whispered, "Mom, I don't think I won an award tonight."

Then she had told him, "You did. You just have to wait."

Pam was not talking about Tim winning an award later on that night at the show. She had said this because his reward will come from God. One day he will be rewarded from the Lord, which is much more important than having rewards here on earth.

This story was so powerful to hear because so many of us get discouraged when we work so hard, doing amazing things. Sometimes, or even most of the time, it goes unnoticed and we are not recognized.

We do not have to be upset about this though, because one day we will be rewarded greatly for the work we do for the Lord. God sees all things and will reward us one day.

He also may reward us through supernatural ways we won't understand. As seen in Genesis, Abraham let Lot choose which piece of divided land he wanted first rather than being selfish and choosing the best before him. God saw how Abraham was not thinking of himself, letting Lot choose first and rewarded him beyond what he would have gotten if he chose what he considered best for himself. The Lord sees all things even when we feel that no one does. Remember His supernatural ways.

We will most definitely be rewarded when we meet with Him again. We will have a special place in heaven with him which he promises if we believe in Him.

The Lord knows your true heart, your true intentions, and the true honest work you do, and for that you will be rewarded one day with him. Do not be discouraged today if you feel you are not rewarded and a lot of what you do goes unnoticed.

Do not feel like you failed if you do not win something, because our greatest reward comes from above. This reward given by the Lord beats anything this earth can grant you. As you obey Him, believe in Him and work for Him.

Your life will be so blessed, and one day you will see and experience this wonderful award of eternal life.

For Colossians 3:23-24 says, "Whatever you do, work at it with all your heart, as working for the Lord, not for human masters, since you know that you will receive an inheritance from the Lord as a reward. It is the Lord Christ you are serving."

It is normal to want to do well and win an award or be noticed for the hard work and talent you put forth. **It's natural to desire to do well. The thing you need to be careful of is idolizing rewards from human masters.**

You are serving Christ, ultimately, so you should be searching and longing to make Him proud. The world cannot do anything for you, and they don't have to. The world is unreliable, so when you are feeling down, unnoticed and not rewarded for your hard work, know that one day you will be rewarded by the Lord for your faithfulness.

Your reward is coming soon, so do not be discouraged. Be patient.

Day 8: Bandages

Every so often we get cuts, scrapes, and different injuries that need bandages. Some people might even get them frequently. Bandages help temporarily fix these injuries we get. They cover the wound but don't heal.

Sometimes they are small, and we just need a bandage for a day or two. Then, other times when we have deep cuts, we can only use bandages for so long until it needs another way to heal. Bandages do not last long. They are not forever. They are small fixes for our injuries. They will cover your injury, your cut, and your scrapes, but they will not heal them. Think of them as only temporary.

Think of alcohol, sex, and drugs, etc., as bandages for the problems we have. Or maybe your bandage takes the form of gambling, excessive shopping, dieting, TV, or changing your hair color constantly. Bandages can take many forms.

These things we may use to make us feel better, just like bandages, will not last forever. They are temporary fixes. They cover the injury up but do not heal them. These bandages, such as alcohol, sex, drugs, shopping, or overeating will not help with the root of your problem. It won't heal your pain. It just temporarily numbs it.

Do not feel discouraged, because we do have one everlasting thing to help us heal and take real care of our problems which is not temporary. The requirement is opening your heart and letting this fix come in.

The Lord is our fix. Invite him into your heart, let him replace your bandages.

If we do not do this and keep using our bandages, those bandages will soon become another problem, perhaps bigger problems. You don't want to be tied up in that mess. Let the Lord heal you. He is not temporary and will only do good. He won't become a problem.

Remember Psalm 147:3, which says, "He heals the broken hearted and binds up their wounds."

Always remember, He heals.

Day 9: Don't Take God's Reins

Every Christmas, I try to make sure I take time in the morning as well as throughout the day to thank God for being a wonderful Father and all that He does, but also to wish Him a happy birthday.

Many people throughout the world may not fully realize or acknowledge that Christmas is the celebration of Jesus Christ's birth. It is still so hard to understand how someone can love us so much that He died for us. So we should absolutely praise the Lord for all of the things He has done for us, especially since we are so undeserving of it.

However, I must admit I do get carried away with the materialistic parts of Christmas. I love the different festivities that go on such as decorating, being with family and friends, giving and receiving gifts, eating great food, and spending time with people I don't get to see often.

I love the classic movies that get you in the holiday spirit, especially when you are a child, such as *Rudolf The Red Nosed Reindeer.* I look forward to watching it each Christmas because it was one of my favorite Christmas movies growing up. It would get me in the spirit and excited about Santa, the North Pole and the reindeer. Honestly, I could probably watch it year round because I think it is the cutest movie.

As most of you know, in this movie it shows us how Santa goes around to each house dropping the presents off through the chimney. His transportation is his famous sleigh. Of course, there are reindeer to pull the sleigh while flying so that he can direct them to every place he needs to go. Because Santa is the one who controls the reins, he will be able to control the path they take. If he wants to land, they listen to him. If he wants to stop or keep going, then they will do just that, unless, of course, they disobey.

So let God take the reins today. Be like Dasher, Dancer, Prancer, Vixen, Comet, Cupid, Donner, Blitzen, and Rudolph. **Let God control where you go, knowing that He has the reins. Obey Him when he tells you to stop or to keep going. Do not try to take your own path when you are blind to where you're going. You don't have the reins—God does. He is the only one with them, so don't try to take them and be in control.**

Psalm 25:4-5 says, "Make me know your ways, LORD, teach me your paths. Guide me in your truth and teach me, for you are God my Savior, and my hope is in you all day long."

As this Psalm says, guide me in your truth and teach me. We need to do just that and wait for the Lord, as His plans are perfect. Do not try to snatch the reins from Him because you will fail. It is best to wait for His perfect timing for His perfect plans.

Take today to think on areas in your life where you need to let go of the reins you stole from Him. Let God take the reins.

Day 10: I do

I love weddings. I grew up thinking all the time about what mine would be like, fantasizing about who my prince would be. As a child, I would even dress up in white gowns and long white gloves pretending to be a bride. I couldn't wait.

Even now, I dream of the day when I will marry the man who sweeps me off my feet. At weddings, it is known that the groom and bride say, "I do" to each other during the ceremony, meaning they do promise to be there in the good times and bad, and sickness and health. Sometimes people go back on that promise and leave when the bad times roll on in, which leaves the other person in devastation or sometimes overall sadness in both cases.

We all know in life there are always going to be good times and there will always be bad times. It is inevitable. Do we still stick by God when bad times come by? Or do we blame Him and turn our backs?

We cannot divorce God when bad times come. That would be like saying, "When I am happy and see You do works in my life, I will praise You, but if something bad happens and I don't understand it, I'm gone."

You can't ditch God. We need to know that He has a special plan for us, even when something bad happens. You don't know what He has in store, so don't divorce Him. Stick to your promise, and stay for sickness and in health. Even though we don't understand it right then and there, He does and promises to never forsake us.

41

I'm not saying it is easy to stand by Him during hard times because it is certainly not, but I can tell you it will be worth it.

I remember reading Tim Tebow's book *Shaken* where he talks about his foundation he has with Christ and how he was let down in certain situations in his life where he had to know that his true identity was not a football player but rather what the Lord says, and how to stand firm with Christ when he was shaken. Like Tim, we need to have a strong foundation and strengthen it every day so that we can stand strong even when we are "shaken."

Not only should we praise and look to God in the good times, but the bad times are when we need Him the most. Don't just say, "I do" to God and choose to believe in him when you're happy, then when something bad happens, you leave faster than a sports car.

Say, "I do" and mean it. Take action on it. Praise Him always, even more in the bad times, for that's when you are learning and strengthening your faith. He knows what He is doing, so have faith even when you don't understand.

Psalm 34:1-3 says it perfectly, "I will extol the Lord at all times; his praise will always be on my lips. I will glorify in the LORD; let the afflicted hear and rejoice. Glorify the LORD with me; let us exalt his name together."

As the Lord is with you through it all and promises to never leave you. Make sure when you say, "I do," you follow through. Praise him through your roughest times and know that He has so much more in store for you.

Day 11: Hold Your Fork High

While I was in Haiti with my Father, driving through Port Au Prince, the man who housed us for the few days told a story. It was quite simple, really, yet unforgettable due to its importance and hopefulness. He told us that a lady in Haiti who was dying had a minister bless her before she passed. This lady said to the minister, "I need a fork in my hand when I go."

The minister asked her why and she replied by saying, "Because after you have dinner and you keep your fork, it means that dessert worth staying for is coming."

It took me a moment to register what that meant, and when it did I was amazed at how this can apply to our lives. This small story showed real hope, something I have never heard before. But most importantly, it showed that through the scariest times, you have something to hope for.

Through the ups and downs in life we should keep this story in mind and remember that there is always something worth waiting for. As this wise lady suggested, there was something to hope for. She was simply showing that her divine appointment with the Lord is something she is waiting for and it's worth it.

The hope that this woman had is impeccably remarkable and powerful, especially to those who are discouraged, feeling like there is nothing to look forward to. This lady was breathing some of her last breaths and speaking some of her last words, yet she was so hopeful for her divine appointment she has with the Lord.

Wait for the dessert that is coming, and hold your fork;

hold it high. Grab a hold of it and don't let go.

The Lord always wants us to hope and trust in Him that He will provide. It does not matter the circumstance you are currently situated in, whether you are going to jail, you are getting a divorce, a horrible health condition, debt, or losing a loved one.

Hold onto your fork. There will always be dessert worth waiting for coming from the Lord. Our dessert is the blessings the Lord has in store for us and it is worth waiting for.

Do not give up in your situation. I know it may seem impossible to get out of, or impossible to smile again, but we don't have to rely on us. God has it. He can do the impossible and He can save you and bring you dessert while you are in the midst of drowning. ·

Job 11:18-19 says, "You will be secure, because there is hope; you will look about you and take your rest in safety. You will lie down, with no one to make you afraid, and many will court your favor."

Hold your fork, and hold it high! For the Lord is waiting to give you what you are unable to possibly imagine. There will always be dessert worth waiting for.

Day 12: Tone Vs. Bulk

I've been told that if you want a long-term effect for toning your muscles, the key is to lift smaller weights and do a lot of reps.

If you lift a lot of weight at a time and only do a few reps, that will make your muscles more bulky, and you will not have as good of a foundation when just starting out.

If you tone your muscles first and build a foundation, then it will last longer, look better, and you'll eventually be able to do more.

I made sure I toned my muscles, so my arms were not bulky, and I had a strong foundation. It worked.

However, there are always people who don't start off by toning their muscles and obtain a good foundation, which results in short-term results.

You are probably thinking: *How is this relevant?* Well, I'm thinking that too... Just kidding, stay with me on this one. It's important.

You can apply this to your life and with your relationship with God.

If you read God's word every day, even just a little bit each day, you will tone your mind.

You will build a great foundation in Christ by learning more about Him. You will know Him much more than before. Listen to what the Bible is saying. Really listen.

If you read half of the Bible all in one sitting then not read again until another month or two, your foundation and knowledge won't last long.

You might even forget everything you ever even read. Your relationship with God won't be as great as it could be. Just like when you are in the gym, if you tone your muscles it will last longer and be more efficient. Tone your mind too. Make God's word stick in your mind. Keep up with the Word, and listen to what it says. You will learn about the merciful God we have.

Mathew 7:24-27 says, "Therefore everyone who hears these words of mine and puts them into practice is like a wise man who built his house on rock. The rain came down, the streams rose, and the winds blew and beat against that house; yet it did not fall, because it had its foundation on the rock. But everyone who hears these words of mine and does not put them into practice is like a foolish man who built his house on sand. The rain came down, the streams rose, and the winds blew and beat against that house, and it fell with a great crash."

Tone yourself in the word, rather than bulking up, so you can experience a long-lasting relationship with Him. Listen to the word from God and learn from it each day so you can live a glorious life and experience His love.

A great foundation in Christ is necessary in this life where we experience brutal storms of adversity and tribulations. When the rain comes down, the streams rise, and the wind blows it is necessary for a firm foundation in Christ to keep from falling down.

Day 13: 1-800 Urgency

Take a minute to think about what in your life would need to be fixed immediately if it was broken. I bet a lot of you would say your phone, car, or maybe your television. I'm guessing a computer or an oven too.

Some of those things listed would need to be fixed urgently, while the others would not. If you didn't have a phone for a few weeks because it broke, and it is the only way people get a hold of you, it would be in urgent need of fixing. When your television breaks, that is something that is not as urgent, since it's not a communication line or survival device. When putting the two in comparison, you would probably pick your phone to be more urgent, since that is something you need more, rather than watching a show or movie on television.

Think about things in your life that are broken and are in urgent need of fixing. Maybe you have anxiety that debilitates your functioning, or relationship problems, health issues, or financial debt. Sometimes we choose to please other people and do other things, like overload our work schedule, or start new projects when there are things in our life in urgent need of fixing.

Which issues in your life are in urgent need of a solution? Start making these problems at the top of your list. Mark them as an urgent need.

Your life is more urgent than the vacation you're trying to plan, or your friend you're trying to please.

As Psalm 50:15 says, "And call on me in the day of trouble; I will deliver you, and you will honor me."

As we have troubles that need immediate attention, we should call on the Lord daily. He will help us, but we need to make sure we treat them as urgent needs and not ignore them. Do not let your problems that need urgent attention linger so they hinder you from the potential the Lord has for you.

Day 14: At War

The first time I went to Washington D.C was with one of my roommates from college and her boyfriend, an officer in the navy. It was a humbling and learning time for all of us.

As I walked through the Arlington cemetery, I observed many different people, some being veterans, family of war heroes, and tourists like myself. As we saw all these different people, I realized they all had one thing in common which was honoring the ones who died fighting for our country.

I started getting emotional as I walked through the cemetery because I saw many war veterans who had survived the war and were now visiting deceased friends and family in that cemetery.

We walked all through the cemetery and then came upon something humbling. I think this was the most emotional time for me there, as I had time to sit and think about the courage these men and women had and have.

As I was sitting in front of the Tomb of the Unknown Soldier waiting to watch the switch of the guards, I started to think about different things like how we as individuals are each at war every day—a spiritual war, that is.

Every day the enemy is attacking our minds, our hearts, and our souls. The enemy wants to destroy our conscience and keep us from getting closer to God.

We must stand together and lean on each other in this war where the devil is attacking us. The Lord tells us that He is all we need, but He is not all we get.

This only means we have family and friends to lean on, to worship with, and encourage one another, especially in God's name. More importantly He gives us people to fight with in this spiritual war we are in, in order to be victorious.

Each day you are being attacked; you have to fight for peace. You are at war with the enemy who is a serpent, the devil.

Do not give up. Buckle up and fight. You are not alone.

2nd Timothy 2:3 says, "Join me in suffering, like a good soldier of Christ Jesus."

Whatever circumstance we are in, and whichever hardship we are dealing with, we must gear up and suffer the hardship with Jesus Christ as well as our brothers and sisters in Christ.

We are in spiritual warfare every day and we are the soldiers of Christ. Every day it is essential for you to wake up and believe you will win the fight the devil put against you.

One powerful verse I hope you remember wherever you go, is Joshua 1:9: "Have I not commanded you? Be strong and courageous. Do not be afraid; do not be discouraged, for the Lord your God is with you wherever you go."

Wherever you are in life, the Lord is in your presence, He's around you and He's watching over you. Whether you are at war, in surgery, stranded somewhere with no signs of hope, you're never alone.

Bring out the fighter in you and conquer the battles the enemy puts in your mind and heart. You can do it, you have the Lord on your side.

I give honor to past, present, and future war heroes.

Day 15: Day Choose Your Home Wisely

As my brother and sister-in-law are looking for a new place to live, a few questions arose for them. One question was why they wanted to rent a house instead of buy one.

They replied by stating, "Well, we are not sure we want to stay here forever, so we want to rent for the time being."

I thought that was wise, but I also thought my brother and sister-in-law could sell their house if they decided to move later on in life, so essentially they could just buy if they wanted to.

This got me thinking about how picking a home to live in and the location is an important decision. Although we are blessed to be able to sell our houses and be able to move to different locations and rent homes and/or apartments, we cannot do that when the time comes and it is too late.

It is so important to think of where our home will be when the Lord returns. We cannot rent or sell our heavenly home like we can here on earth. When we decide to be with the Lord and never turn from Him, then our home will be in heaven. If we decide to not be with Him or turn from Him, then our home will not be in heaven and there will not be a way to change that when it is too late.

If we are not at home with the Lord in Heaven when our time comes, we can't just move over with him and everything will be fine. There is no moving, renting, or leasing with him.

Our eternal home is permanent. We must choose wisely, now, right this second, because we are placed in our home forever when the time comes. Do not turn from God as He wants you to be with Him in His Kingdom when the time comes. Believe in the Lord and choose Him so you may have eternal life.

We really are so blessed with an amazing God because He promises if we believe in Him, we will endure in His home forever. That is so amazing.

Once we are in His home, we are there forever. We will never move.

We will have peace always, and there will be no pain and no sin. Imagine no heartache.

He set aside a special place for us, so we can be with Him forever. Doesn't that make you smile?

Choose now to believe in God, because He wants you with Him forever. But you must remember, anything unfortunate can happen without being able to prepare. If unfortunate events do happen and you didn't accept the Lord before passing away, it will be too late.

For John 3:16 says, "For God so loved the world that he gave his one and only Son, for whoever believes in Him shall not perish but have eternal life."

The most wonderful gift you will ever receive is that God loves you so much He gave His only Son to die for us, so we do not have to suffer and die for our sins. He loves us so much He constantly gives us a choice to believe in Him, so we can have eternal life in heaven. He doesn't want us to perish and suffer which is why he gives us the choice to believe in Him and be with Him.

Choose your home wisely, and choose God, for He will bring you to your eternal home in heaven when the time comes. He promises you will not perish but have eternal life.

John 14:2-4 says, "My Father's house has many rooms; if that were not so, would I have told you that I am going there to prepare a place for you? And if I go and prepare a place for you, I will come back and take you to be with me that you also may be where I am. You know the way to the place where I am going."

The Lord is telling us we know the way, which is Him. If we follow Him and believe in Him, we will be with Him forever. There are rooms prepared for us, so choose now.

Day 16: Shoulder to Shoulder

It can be really frustrating and hard to understand someone who does not speak the same language as you, especially when you are trying to ask a question or just say something important, but you can't. I have encountered this on many different occasions, although in Haiti, it was the most difficult.

It was definitely a time where I really wished I was fluent in Creole, because there were a lot of language barriers. Even though this was quite frustrating, because I couldn't communicate a lot of the times what I wanted to say, I learned later on that I was communicating at times when nothing was being said through body language.

There was a time in Haiti when I was required to hike up a mountain in order to get to a village, and one of the Haitians we were with helped me without being asked, pretty much the entire time. It was like I had a nanny. After a few hours, we headed back down the mountain to get to where our vehicle was. This time around, it was raining pretty hard, which made it even more difficult to get down, since everything was muddy, and the rocks were so slippery. The same man helped me down the mountain without me asking and was so gracious with me. I was scared, and I think most people could see it in my eyes as I thought for sure, there was no way I was going to make it down this mountain.

As I slipped, constantly dragging him with me because he was holding my arm the entire time, he never once got frustrated with me. He knew very well I was not used to this.

It took about an hour and a half to finally reach the bottom, and we barely spoke the entire time. Exchanging only a few words during that time span (considering he mainly only spoke Creole), especially for a talker like me and in a scary situation, sounds like an awful time, but for me I learned and realized that it was something I needed. It was the exact thing I didn't want, but God knew I needed it.

Although we didn't speak much, I could feel God's love through him. He was patient, selfless, and very kind when I was a lot to handle. Even though he couldn't say much to me, and I couldn't say much to him, I could feel the love through his actions.

There were also a few moments when we both laughed even though it was pouring, and we were struggling to get down the mountain through a rocky and muddy stream, I was struggling. We didn't think it would rain on our way back.

There was nothing that was said except simple words like "okay" and "yes" or "no" but we could communicate through emotions. When we laughed, it was because I would slip constantly and have to hold his hand the whole time, even in easy spots.

We would just look at each other and laugh, because we both knew, for me, it was not an ideal situation, and I was definitely not equipped for it.

Without exchanging words to each other, we could sense the emotion we had and make the best of it. Through his actions I could feel and see Jesus' shining light through him.

God created many different languages that people speak, and sometimes it's extremely frustrating to not be able to comprehend what others are saying, but other times it's so beautiful because you can exchange what you want to say through actions and emotions.

The Unfinished Puzzle   Ashley Alice White

As the Lord tells us that He is all we need, because He will provide everything and sustain us, He doesn't say He is all we get.

Even though God is everything that can comfort us and give us peace, He gives us friends and family to be with and support us, even when they do not speak the same language or have the same views.

I didn't know the Lord would show me His love and kindness, as well as true peace and joy, through a scary time overseas. He constantly sends people our way to teach us and to give us joy, even when we don't understand.

Another time I witnessed this was when I saw my dad and the pastor of the village of Pavillon share their love of God to one another. They prayed together, both in different languages, which was not understood by everyone but we all felt the presence of the Lord.

The entire village, as well as my father and I, could sense and feel the love that the Lord supplied us with to share together and help one another.

As the Lord says, He is not all we get, and this is a perfect example of that.

A lady who was with us and would often translate told us that even though they can't understand us, they were so appreciative we were there to help and that we brought them so much hope.

Even if we can't understand each other through speaking, the love Jesus gives us can be shown through one another even when words are not always exchanged. And sometimes these actions truly are louder than words.

God intended for us to love one another, even if we have differences and have different cultures. As He helped many people in need, and loved on everyone, He wants us to do the same. Sometimes the Lord can show his love through people to shed on you, which is what I felt throughout the entire trip.

Listen to what Zephaniah 3:9 says: "Then I will purify the lips of the peoples, that all of them may call on the name of the LORD and serve him shoulder to shoulder."

When we put the differences of language, culture, and all views aside, we all share the same love that Jesus shows us. We are to serve together, shoulder to shoulder.

Show love to someone today, even if you don't understand them. The Lord gives us peace, hope, love, joy, and faith to experience for ourselves, but to also be a light for someone else.

Have hope in the fact that you can always see the light of Jesus, and sometimes it is shown through someone else, or through an incredibly frightening time.

Stand shoulder to shoulder, and praise the Lord together.

Day 17: Don't Confuse the Two

Sometimes we are over-focused and set on just one thing which causes us to close our minds and hearts to opportunities. We want what we want, so if anything else comes our way that is not what we think we want, we deny it.

We can be so selfish and picky this way because we're flawed. I do this all the time and end up missing out because I'm so set on the one thing and think what I want is what I need. A lot of the time the thing I want doesn't work out because I'm not looking at the entire picture.

There are so many times this happens when I obsess over something I think I need and there will be nothing that can change my mind. I would pray to God to bless me with this one thing I think I want and neglect to ask Him for His will.

When the thing I asked for doesn't happen, I get angry. I become frustrated and think the Lord failed me.

Thinking of this now, it's silly to think the Lord is failing me, but at the time of these disappointments, I was devastated and crushed. I blamed everything on God, claiming He doesn't follow through and never helps me.

I thought He did everything for everyone else, blessing them abundantly, while I sat in misery praying for things I wanted and not receiving them.

Why would he follow through if it wasn't His will or plan in the first place? I wasn't listening to Him, and I wasn't following His path He set out for me. I didn't even ask Him for the direction for His plan, and I didn't ask for His will. I simply asked what I thought I wanted without including him.

I confused failure with God's plan. How many times do we do this? A lot of us do it without even knowing it.

We think we are doing well by praying to God, asking and seeking. But are we actually seeking? Seeking is looking for God's perfect plan and asking Him for that, not the ungodly things we want because those certainly won't come from the Lord.

We need to make sure we really understand how God works, not only in the way of how He makes things happen or how He creates, but in terms of our relationship with Him. He knows us better than we know ourselves.

You may ask, and He may say no, but He doesn't say no without a reason behind it. When He says no, we fail to understand that there's a reason, such as God having something far more significant in store.

Looking back at the things I pleaded and begged God for, thinking those were the only things I wanted and I wouldn't be happy otherwise, I'm now thrilled because for the most part I see why God said no or told me it wasn't the right time for many things I asked for not aligning with His will.

Now I don't want most of those things at all. I am a different person than before, and what God has given me is far better than what I asked for.

He knows us so much more than we think we know ourselves, and

He knows what we need. He created us, so He knows the way our brains function, and He knows what our heart beats for.

He knew all along that I would change my mind and that I wouldn't want to be where I asked to be, or who I asked to be with. He protected me from the things I thought I wanted.

He didn't fail me, I just confused what I thought was failure with His plan. I also confused failure with His protection, because I didn't understand why He was saying no to some of the things I wanted. He protected me from a dark road.

It is normal to not understand what He is doing, as most of the time we will never understand. We have to have complete faith that He has a divine plan so unique and special, otherwise we're left with our own plans that fail.

Know that if something didn't work out, the Lord has something better. You have more coming. Be patient and trust in the Lord.

Do not confuse His plan and His protection with Him failing you.

John 8:32 says, "Then you will know the truth, and the truth will set you free."

Know the truth. Know that God didn't forget you or fail you. He loves you. This will set you free and give you peace in knowing He is working on your plan. He is making way for your future and protecting you from what you think you want. Remember who the author of true love is, and the designer of the world. Be hopeful today.

Day 18: Dreadful Tunnel

I think of the Chesapeake Bay Bridge in Virginia Beach as the long, dreadful, narrow, dark bridge.

Driving through the tunnel (which is in the middle of the bridge) with your family is not so bad so long as you don't have to be the one driving and everyone is talking with the music ludicrously loud.

It is even worse when you are alone because you start to think of the worst-case scenarios. Not to mention, as you look side to side before you enter the tunnel, it can become overwhelming because you see big bodies of water and all the different vehicles zipping by you while looking side to side.

The bridge is long and quite tedious. When you look around, your terror becomes more realistic. While going through this narrow, dark tunnel, there are vehicles coming the other way, close to skimming your car.

It is a long and dark tunnel that is dreadful, especially alone and at night.

When you go through this tunnel, you look forward to the light you're constantly searching for which indicates that you are reaching the end of the tunnel—that you are close to the end. It is an indication that your destination is coming.

Once the light appears, even the slightest bit, you start to only pay attention to that. You don't even think of the terror and scenarios you created in your mind while in the dark. You strive to get there as efficiently possible. You become determined as soon as there is the tiniest hint of even a glimpse of light appears.

While inevitably going through the dark, horrid tunnels we have to go through in some parts of our lives, we can strive every day to see the light which comes from the Lord. If you spot the smallest glimpse of light in your life, strive to get there.

Act as if you are in the tunnel, staying in your lane and focusing on nothing else but that sight of hope.

Don't look back. You are moving forward only. Look forward to the places you will go.

God gives us a future, so we don't have to dwell in our past! He secures our future and provides a way out of our past. Every day we need to look for the light, to find our destination that God set out for us.

Do not pull over to the side or look at any other cars going through that tunnel, or you might veer and hit another car. Distractions are not acceptable. Pay attention and get yourself ready and focused for the sighting of light, your indication of hope.

Get yourself safely through the tunnels of darkness we will go through in life. When you are going through a tunnel and you think there is no way out, hold on to the fact that the Lord promises us a way out. You just need faith.

"The LORD is my light and my salvation—whom shall I fear? The LORD is the stronghold of my life—of whom shall I be afraid?" -Psalm 27:1

The Lord is your light, so there shall be no fear, and no one to be

The Unfinished Puzzle   Ashley Alice White

afraid of.

Day 19: Hydrate Yourself

Do you ever get so busy that you forget to actually drink water throughout the day? What happens when we do that? For starters, we become weak and sick due to dehydration.

I usually have so much water throughout the day to make sure those things don't happen, because I'll become irritated and not feel good, and so I try to prevent that. Though, sometimes it happens because I get busy and forget.

When I went to England, the second time around, I was feeling really sick because I didn't drink as much water as I usually do. I didn't know why I felt sick until it clicked that I wasn't drinking my usual eight glasses a day, since I was so busy unpacking, meeting new people and going to orientation. Instead I was averaging barely 3 glasses. I knew I was dehydrated.

When we lack the Word of God, the same thing happens.

We are not as strong as we were; we become weak and sick. The Word is the water of life. We may need at least 10 glasses of water a day to keep our bodies hydrated, but we need the everlasting Word of God to keep our hearts, minds, and souls hydrated.

Just like needing water in order to live, we need God's Word to truly live.

To live free and not be in the bondage of our sins, we have to hydrate ourselves in the Word of God to constantly know Him, be encouraged, and live

according to His Word.

John 7:38 says, "Whoever believes in me, as scripture has said, rivers of living water will flow from within them."

If we believe in Him, we can enjoy the fountain of good as well as the love He has. We need to stay hydrated in the Word, so we can truly know this and follow His steps and be full of joy and constantly hopeful.

Day 20: Prerequisites

Remember being in high school? Or if you are in high school, you'll get this.

Before you took a certain class there were—and are—prerequisites, which meant you had to take a class before the one you wanted to take. I definitely remember it because I could never get into the classes I wanted, considering there were always required prerequisites before those classes I wanted to take.

All I wanted to do was take certain classes right when I wanted to, creating my own perfect schedule. Although, it didn't work that way, considering you have to follow the rules and take the prerequisites.

Before you get the good class, you have to take the not-so-good class to make sure you are ready for the one you want. You have to take prerequisites to prepare yourself for the real thing.

Think of problems as prerequisites for miracles. This means you have to have a problem before you have a miracle. How could we have miracles if there are no problems in need of a miracle?

You might not understand the problem that you have now, but there will be a miracle in the end. The problem has to happen in order for the miracle to come—a problem or trial is the prerequisite.

If a miracle has to happen, then there may be a problem that comes first so God can give you the amazing miracle you're praying for, even if it seems impossible.

Nothing glorious or amazing would happen if there were no problems to be resolved, which only goes to show that problems are prerequisites for miracles.

When we have problems, of course it's irritating. No one wants to have problems, but we can change the way we think about them. I know it is difficult, but it is possible.

I don't think anyone will ever like problems, and since that is the case, we can have a positive mindset about moving on from them rather than settling with them. It sounds cookie-cutter and cliché, but I promise it's not.

Instead of dwelling upon the negative issues we have in our life, we should ask God what He wants us to do next and thank him for the miracle we know He will perform that comes after our problems.

If a problem comes our way, and we have God in our hearts, you know He has a miracle heading your way, because He never wastes pain! Think positively about your problems because a miracle is coming your way. When I say "miracle," I am not just talking about supernatural things happening. You may not know what your miracle is or know that it happened, but know now that the Lord has a plan for you and will not waste your pain.

Instead of sulking about all the issues in your life, praise God for the supernatural God He is and thank Him for seeing you through it.

Naaman, a man from the Bible with horrible leprosy, thought he would never be healed. He was told strange instructions from a servant to dip himself in the Jordan River seven times, and he would be healed. As it didn't really make sense, he still followed the instructions and did as he was asked. He did this, and a miracle happened. Naaman's skin became as smooth as ever.

Sometimes the things God tells us to do won't make sense to us because we can't fathom how He does the things He does, but we have to trust that He has a special plan for everything. We are not asked to understand but to believe and obey, so believe in the miracle headed your way!

As we now know, problems are prerequisites for miracles. Start changing the way you think about them, because victory is coming to you. Stay positive and praise the Lord for His greatness.

As Exodus 15: 26 says, He said, "If you listen carefully to the LORD your God and do what is right in his eyes, if you pay attention to his commands and keep all his decrees, I will not bring on you any of the diseases I brought on the Egyptians, for I am the LORD, who heals you."

Remember there is hope for everything and every situation. He tells us He can heal us. Get praying today and remember to believe and obey! Something better is coming.

Day 21: Preparing for Company

Before company would come over, even family and really close friends, my mother would run around the house making sure everything was clean and tidy. She had to make sure everything was immaculate before anyone came to visit.

My dad hated this time before any family party we hosted, solely because of my mom freaking out beforehand. We would all help her but didn't do as good as a job she would. I do admit I was this way too as I was growing up, just not to her extent, making sure before my friends came over that my room was clean and looked nice.

When you really think about it, you start to question why we even do that. Our family and friends know how we live, and they know things get messy and out of order. Of course if your home is extremely messy you would clean it, but I'm talking about when it's already clean and we do so much that it looks like no one lives, like it's brand new.

Everyone who knows us knows we don't prance around our house all day, tip-toeing around, keeping the house in tip-top condition at all times.

Let's be realistic. We spill coffee, we throw the towels on the floor, and the floors get dirty, especially with pets and kids. It is inevitable.

Do you do this in your life with God?

Do you treat God like company? Do you try to clean up everything that seems "messy" and unclean before letting God in?

He wants to be there to help you and listen to what you have to say about your messy life. He already knows your every thought and your every move, because He created you.

Why are you trying to pretend there are no messes in your life when He already sees them? Sometimes people feel like they are too messy or not good enough, maybe even have too much baggage to be with God, but that is not true because He already sees everything. He knows everything about us; we are not too messy for Him.

We shouldn't treat Him like company and clean everything up before we talk to Him and let Him enter our hearts. He is not there to hear you pretend you're not a mess without Him—He wants you to confess that you are a mess, so He can help you.

He wants to clean you, so you don't need to. Let Him see the mess.

John 10:14 "I am the good shepherd; I know my sheep and my sheep know me."

The Lord knows everything about us. So don't feel like you need to clean up your life before letting Him enter. As He knows us, we will know Him.

Invite God into your real life and your messy, coffee-spilling, dirty-floored, messy-laundry home. Do not feel like you are too messy for Him. There is nothing He cannot handle.

Day 22: Face God

I was lying in bed, facing the same white wall I had been looking at since I was nine years old, tears streaming down my face, questioning myself and perhaps even God my senior year of high school, so I was most likely 17 or 18 years old.

Is this really it? This is my life? This is why I was created, to settle? This is your big plan, huh? I prayed.

I had been rejected by every college I applied to in my senior year of high school. I tried to act like I was fine and as if I was not upset at all, but I was truly embarrassed that I managed to not get into one school I applied to. I didn't apply to colleges that were difficult to get into so it wasn't because of that. It wasn't because of my grades either. I had a little below-average SAT score, which is not uncommon, because it was about the same as many of my friends. I was left confused and heartbroken.

My parents were probably more heartbroken than I was, just knowing how horrible it is to be rejected, especially while all your friends are being accepted and excited.

Getting the last letter of rejection was when I returned back to the white wall. Every time it seemed like my world deteriorated, I would face that white wall.

I couldn't believe I was there, in that position again. I thought: *What will I do? How awful it will be, staying home while my friends leave.*

What would be even worse than those things is the fact I was in that position again, blankly staring at the same wall as I had done so many other bleak times before.

I remember that feeling of being rejected and the heartbreak that overcomes your sense of identity.

I don't have to face that white wall again. This time around that when my world seems to fall apart, it's not that wall that I turn to.

I face God.

The Lord showed me his plans were far beyond what I expected and ever imagined once I faced Him and sought what He was planning.

As I started at a community college, then moved to a university, He brought me abroad to one of the greatest schools in the world, a place I would never expect.

I went to the University of Oxford, located in England, for a summer semester I studied writing and English. For someone who was rejected at first by every college applied to, imagine doing this. Before being accepted, I wrote an essay while knowing my grade point average wasn't exactly impressive hoping for the best with recommendations, or course. Weeks after I not only got the news of acceptance that day but a newfound confidence too.

I had to immediately praise God once I was accepted because I knew this was His plan all along. He didn't want me to go to those other colleges because I would have never gone to Oxford. I wouldn't have ended up applying there. As there are many different study-abroad programs throughout the world, the only one the university I went to and go to now offered in England was that one. If I had gone to another college, perhaps the ones I wanted to go too, I most likely would have never applied to the

University of Oxford because I thought of it as out of my league, until it became my only choice so I took the risk.

God will provide and He will show you the way. After a few years, I finally realized why He said "no" and "not yet" when I applied to a bunch of different schools He didn't want me at.

We cannot doubt God because He truly knows what is best for us, even when we feel He is not doing anything.

I couldn't understand what He was doing when I was being rejected, left with the feeling of stupidity. I had to wait patiently to see the bigger picture.

I am so glad He said no and didn't allow what I wanted to happen because what He planned exceeded far more than I could have imagined or even thought of.

When facing troubles, discouragement, and worst of all, rejection, face God. Do not doubt Him. He has something beyond your imagination in the works. Don't face anything but Him. You can try and be on your own for so long, but you'll soon see only the God of this universe can make miracles happen.

Isaiah 43:2 says, "When you pass through the waters, I will be with you; and when you pass through the rivers, they will not sweep over you. When you walk through the fire, you will not be burned; the flames will not set you ablaze."

We will walk through water and fire in our lifetime, but we don't have to walk it alone.

Face God.

Day 23: Ascend

There is a five-letter word that most people find problems with. The thought of it, and sometimes even hearing it, scares people away.

A lot of the time, people can't do it, and it ruins relationships because without this scary thing, it is impossible to have a strong relationship.

It's like we were scarred so deeply that it's impossible, in our minds, to take action on this five-letter word and apply it to our lives.

Being close and loyal to someone is a prerequisite to participate with this little word that we find so scary. It is an absolute must in every relationship you are in for it to be successful and happy. I often wonder why we are so scared of this word? Is it the actual word or the memories that come along with it? Maybe it's the hard work put into it, or maybe it's the disappointment it in most cases inevitably brings.

That word is *trust*.

I can almost hear the sigh from every person who just read that. So, think with me. What is so scary about this word? Is it the memory or is it the disappointment? Is it the hard work? A lot of things take hard work.

I'm guessing it's both memories and disappointment. Memories of trusting someone only to have them fail you time and time again is what scares us as well as the disappointment that it brings where you never want to associate with trusting again.

I know you might have been let down so many times and maybe refuse to try again. You are done with it; you broke up with it. You might have moved on from it.

I get it.

Let's do a new thing with this word and associate it with the word, *faith*. If you have faith in God, He will renew this scary word for you.

It doesn't have to be so scary.

Come on, you can do it. This time will be significantly different. Trusting in someone you are friends with, someone you love, or your family is a whole different ball game. Since we are all human, we will make mistakes; there is not much we can do about it. They can—and will—let you down, even if it is in the smallest way. That is why we are here facing this word.

I'll tell you now, trusting in God is easy and hard at the same time. A lot of you probably know that. When you have faith in the Lord and know that He will always come through, it is so much easier to trust in Him. Always associate the word *trust* with *faith* when it comes to God.

It is easy because God does not leave us, He does not wrong us, and He does not lie to us. The one thing the Lord cannot do is wrong us. He is nothing but love.

You will never be hurt by God, and if you think you are, it's because what you want doesn't align with what He has planned for you.

It is easy to trust Him because you know He will never do wrong to you since His love is perfect and unconditional. There are no conditions as to why He loves you. He commends it.

Here comes the hard part. You will feel abandoned at times, but this has nothing to do with him, just you and the enemy. The Lord's timing is not always what we want, because what we want is not always right or in the right time, therefore you may feel as if he left you while you're waiting on his time.

His timing requires much patience. You have to have faith He is still here even when you think that He left. Remind yourself He is working hard during your trials even though you can't see it. However, you cannot go by sight, otherwise you will see nothing and become discouraged, but if you walk by faith you will see everything. You need to know and remind yourself daily that you are always accompanied by God. Trust and have faith that He's with you.

As you move forward, be prepared to learn a whole new level and realm of trust that comes from God. This short and scary word you want nothing to do with now will become your soul mate and your favorite action yet.

Cheers to you for traveling to this next part. You're getting closer and closer to your destination. Do not allow any fear along the way while you ascend to your destination.

Day 24: Seduced By Success

A lot of people think that a title you are given is who you are. However, a title is what you earn from the journey and hard work you put forth.

A title does not define you, your hard work does even when you do not have a title to match it.

There will always be a better rank and a better status— what you have now will never be enough, something and someone else will achieve better.

It is the same with cars. There are constantly new cars always coming out. The one you have now is not going to be the newest edition in a few months, I'm sure.

I'm not proud of this, but my mindset had been that once I achieve this or get that I'll be happy, and once I obtain a new success or save this much money I'll settle down and be satisfied. However, I've learned it doesn't stop there, because once I obtain all those things, there is something else that comes along as well as someone else who will do what I did, but better.

I learned the hard way that it doesn't satisfy you, and I was seduced by the temporary happiness it brings.

Don't be seduced by success.

Fancy titles, large amounts of success, and money are quite seductive. They look and sound great, seeming like they are all you need, but you'll never be satisfied with all that the world brings.

You will keep wanting and chasing more. Do not try and satisfy yourself with success, money, or titles. Don't be seduced by it.

Let yourself be known by who you are in Christ and what title God gives you, his precious child. He says you are His son or you are His daughter. You are his precious child and more than enough. **Sure, it's great to be successful and want to better yourself every day, which you absolutely should, but be careful with idolizing the success you obtain and the feeling of wanting to chase it more. It brings you down a dark road.**

Mathew 6:21 tells us, "For where your treasure is, there your heart will be also."

This is telling us that what you admire and what makes you happy (your treasure) there your heart will be.

Do not let that treasure be success, let it be God.

He can bring you success once you delight yourself in Him! He wants to prosper you, so don't idolize anything but Him.

He will provide for all your needs as He knows your desires and exactly what you need. Do not be seduced by the world, or you'll become a victim of a constant chase you can't keep up with where what you obtain will never be enough.

Exodus 20:3 "You shall have no other God's before me."

Speaking of idolizing, the Lord strictly tells us there shall be no other God's before him. While many may think this means other gods such as the ones other religions worship, it also speaks upon things and people we may idolize, such as money, cars, men or women, clothes, and success.

The Lord should be our only focus, the only God we turn to and trust. We cannot idolize success and look at it as our God. He is the only one who will bring you happiness, peace, and true success without feeling overwhelmed from the chase. Do not make the chase of titles, money, women, or men your life.

Be in the Word constantly so you find a life full of joy where the Lord provides for all your needs and wants. Be patient and trust that He has this.

Day 25: All Nighters

The first time I planned my own vacation was when I went to Jamaica with my best friend. It was the first time I was leaving the country by myself with just a friend as well as planning it by myself.

I had to make sure we both had the same flights and connecting flights. I had to make sure our room and transportation to and from the resort was set up perfectly, so we could get everywhere on time and didn't miss our rides throughout the trip. It was time consuming and tedious, but it had to be done in order to make sure everything worked out as planned.

Meeting the people we meet, getting the jobs we get, and with everything we do—there has to be a perfect plan the Lord sets out for us, even when it seems messy.

Just like when you go on a vacation, it takes time to make sure that you have your times correct, your rides secured and rooms all set. This way everything works out before we reach our destination, which was the resort in Jamaica.

Sometimes things happen and there are delays, such as a taxi being in traffic, a flight being delayed or an accidental overbooking of a hotel. When this happens, it takes even more time to get to where you need to be because of these unfortunate events.

The Lord is setting up appointments and schedules for you to meet your future husband or your wife in his perfect timing if you're not married yet and want to be. He's doing the same thing for your purpose and the career you're meant for, whether you are starting over or not, which may mean a new path or new person for you aligned in His path.

Sometimes there are delays because we don't listen to Him or we disobey and do what we want to do rather than what He says. The result is that our journey takes a bit longer than we'd like.

Maybe you take a job the Lord told you not to take, and this delays your real purpose in life because you didn't listen in the first place, for example.

The Lord has to schedule divine meetings for certain people to meet so everything works out in your favor. He has a plan, and it takes time to get there, because you have to do certain things and meet certain people. For instance, maybe you go on a mission trip and realize that's what you like to do with your life rather than go to law school or medical school. You may meet the love of your life in the field.

Sometimes unfortunate things happen to us because it's part of the plan to get you to where you have to go.

Maybe you had to have surgery and met someone in the hospital you were supposed to meet which changed your life.

Remember, the Lord works in supernatural ways. Sometimes we are confused and think our life is ruined and our "big break" is taking too long to come, or it will never come. However, we need to remember everything has to be scheduled accordingly, so we find our purpose and reach our destination. However, we do have free will where we are able to choose different paths to take, which is why we need to follow the Lord always so that we do not delay our plan He set out for us.

Sometimes there are delays because the person you are supposed to marry didn't listen to God and moved away or was with someone else, or vice versa.

It doesn't mean His plan won't work out for you. It just means He has to make certain things happen and schedule certain divine meetings for people so lessons are learned and their purpose is reached.

Do not get discouraged. Everything He has planned for you is in the works of the Most High God we serve. He is not forgetting you. It is just in His time, not yours.

You have to go through what He has for you right now, so you can meet who you need to meet, and go where you need to go in order to reach what you're created for.

The Lord is working diligently. He is pulling all-nighters to make sure your future is planned and secured. Trust in him. The Bible never says for us to worry, doubt, be anxious, or sad.

Instead, over and over again, it says to trust the Lord.

John 5:17 says, "Jesus said to them, 'My Father is always at his work, to this very day, and I, too, am working.'"

Never doubt the significance of your trials, because they are what lead you to where God wants you to be.

He is always working in supernatural ways, lining up every last important detail for His plans. He tells us he has plans for us, but we must obey and follow His way. When we don't do this, it delays what He had for us, but don't be discouraged. You and I are sinners which means from time to time unfortunately we will disobey, but this doesn't mean He leaves us and says, "never mind, I don't have a plan anymore."

No, it just means it will take longer because there is now a delay to the original intent. We have to learn from not following what He says. Just as we have to schedule every last tedious detail of the trips we take to secure that we get to our destination, the Lord does the same. He works out certain situations to make sure everything works out, but since we do have free will to choose, that is why certain unfortunate things happen. It is not the Lord because he is perfect in all of his way, it is us not choosing the wisely the path to take.

Have hope today because the Lord is working all day and all night on the plan He has for your life. He never gives up on you and will always see you through, even through delays.

Day 26: Rock Climbing

Eighth grade, I believe, was the first time I went rock climbing which was more of a beginners' course. It was located outside in the back of our middle school, close to the track. Our entire eighth grade class had to do it.

You would think everyone would be excited, which most were, but I was more scared of it. I used to be fearless with everything like that until I became scared of heights, which I don't recall when or exactly why.

I really didn't want to rock climb because I knew myself. I knew that I would get up there and not be able to come down or look ridiculous because I couldn't do it.

Essentially, I came up with all the cliché excuses. Typical young girl reasons, I guess. Anyway, I do remember our gym teacher telling us that when we rock climb, we need someone supporting us and showing us how.

We were taught that when someone supported us with ropes and gear, he or she needed to pay attention and make sure we were held up there firmly, but not so firm that we couldn't climb.

Also, we were shown a little bit of a tutorial of how to do this so that we were safe and successful before we went ahead and started. We were told that it was necessary that we not give our climber too much slack with their ropes, and if you were me, you were scared as to why. If they were given too much slack, then they wouldn't be safe, especially if they fell. What a dangerous nightmare that would have been falling from such a high point.

When you are climbing to your destination in life for the purpose God created you for, you should make sure the slack is a good amount, but the support is focused and strong. You need a firm supporter. Make sure the person supporting you knows the right amount that you need, otherwise they are not a good fit.

You should not be near anyone who brings you down, discourages you, and does not look out for your best interest. You need strong supporters only. Slackers in your life who supposedly support you are no longer welcome.

While you're climbing every day in life you can't have too much slack or you could fall.

Be with those who encourage you from God's word, enlighten you in His Spirit, and who love you through any circumstance. Be with the people who support you endlessly through your climb in life.

When you slip or take a wrong step, you don't want to fall. You need a focused support system. Be careful on who those people are, because some might want you to fall.

Ecclesiastes 4:9-12 says, "Two are better than one, because they have a good return for their labor: If either of them falls down, one can help the other up. But pity anyone who falls and has no one to help them up. Also, if two lie down together, they will keep warm. But how can one keep warm alone? Though one may be overpowered, two can defend themselves. A cord of three strands is not quickly broken."

Remember this, "If either of them falls down, one can help the other up."

Watch closely who lifts you up when you slip. It will determine who makes the cut to be your supporters or not. Be wise with your companions and keep the ones who truly enlighten you.

Day 27: Follow the Leader

Follow the leader was such a classic game my family and I would always play. I remember it always being a camping tradition where my sister, dad, and I would play that and "Mother May I" which was another fun game we loved. My sister and I would always look forward to playing these games all together on our camping trips as it was our daddy-daughter camping trip, so my mother and my brother didn't come, as they had on different trips.

When you play follow the leader, as most of you know, the whole point of the game is to follow what the chosen leader does and do whatever they say, otherwise you lose. If they skip around in a circle, then you have to skip around in a circle. Let's say the leader decided to gallop like a horse or sprint like an Olympian, then we must do exactly as they do, and in some occasions, what they say.

Sometimes it is silly stuff that we don't want to do, or stuff we don't like in general, but we do it because we don't want to lose the game, so we just obey.

Take a deeper look into this game and try to apply it to your life. God is the ultimate leader in our lives. He will never make us look silly or do anything that would put us in a bad situation. Like the game follow the leader we may not always want to do as the leader says, but with God, we know what He says is always in our best interest, therefore we should always follow Him and never disobey. It can be hard trying to figure out what He is saying, but you will know if something or someone is from God is it aligns with His word, otherwise it is not from Him or what He would want.

Although, beware, you may be tempted to stray. You might also be discouraged on where He is bringing you until you know why, but don't give in—just trust. When you are discouraged while following the Lord, get in the Word and ask Him for strength to follow Him.

We should strive to be like our Leader more and more each day and follow His leadership. In life, we may be given the opportunity to be a leader, maybe in a job or in a church and when we have that opportunity, we must make sure we are being a good leader acting as Jesus would.

When I was probably about nine or ten years old, we moved to Maine. I was at church where my father preached where I heard for the first time the saying, "What Would Jesus Do?"

Whenever we are facing challenges and have to make important, tough decisions, we should ask that question to ourselves and even others. What would He do? When leading people wherever we are, we need to make sure we are following the ultimate leader and striving to be like Him each and every day. Show His example of leadership in whatever position you are in.

Psalm 37:23 says, "The LORD makes firm the steps of the one who delights in him;."

As our steps are ordered by the Lord, we must make sure we follow each and every step He has for us because we know His way is perfect.

Day 28: Did You Forget Me?

Most of you have probably heard of mothers and fathers accidentally leaving their children at a store because they somehow forgot about them from being so busy. Maybe you are a mother or father who has done that, or worse, maybe you are the child who was forgotten.

There was a time when I was working at a restaurant, where there was a mother who frantically came inside saying she lost her child.

How could the mother have lost her child?

A few minutes later the child was found by a police officer who saw her roaming by herself outside, alone. Sometimes it just happens that people get so involved with what they are doing that they forget, and sometimes it just so happens that we forget people.

It's so easy to do it if you are not paying attention and if you are stressed. People usually don't mean to forget us, but they do because they're not perfect and make mistakes.

If you have ever been forgotten by someone, you know how horrible it feels. I have had times when I tell myself I will call my friend or family back later, but I don't because I forget. It's not that I don't want to, because it could be someone I think so highly of, but I just plain old forget.

That feeling we get when we're forgotten we will never have to feel with the Lord. He won't ever forget us. We may think He does, because we don't understand what He is doing in the moment, but you will see He works diligently all of the time.

There was a time all my friends were having good things happen to them and I wasn't. I was being the most obedient I've been before, and trusting God, but didn't see a single thing happen to me.

I was mad because I thought: *These people are not serving you, Lord, and they mock your name. Why are they being blessed? I am serving you, I am being obedient, and I am believing in you, constantly praising your name.*

It's not that I wasn't happy for my friends, because I love them and love to see them happy, but I was getting impatient with my life and God. I felt as if God forgot about me, so I started to doubt Him, which insults Him.

I was upset and feeling hopeless about my circumstance so I prayed to God, asking Him to show me something, so I would know He didn't forget me. It took me a while to pray this prayer because I was mad at Him.

It is a hard, hard thing to do when you are mad with how things are going in your life, yet praise the Lord. It is so easy to praise God when life is good.

Anyway, He showed me once I prayed hard and it seemed like a little sign of Him telling me He is still there and not forgetting me.

I was amazed how He worked. I still can't understand it, and I know I never will, but I learned to thank God every day for the supernatural things He does. I was feeling forgotten by God because nothing seemed to be going well for me while it was the opposite for everyone around me. I prayed asking God to show me that He is still there and hasn't forgotten me. I prayed that He would show me, even in the smallest way, that He was working on my plan. After that, as I wiped my tears, I was notified that my book was going to be published. I was overwhelmed with joy and praised God and even apologized to Him too because I doubted him originally. I thought He left me and I thought He forgot me. I was reminded how great His love and how strong His power is in that moment. He showed me He is still here, working hard.

Our parents may have forgotten us in stores, or we may forget about the water boiling while we're cooking, or maybe we even forget the dogs are outside—but good news! God never forgets us.

If you are feeling forgotten by Him, ask yourself if you are being patient or not. If you are rushing something, don't. His timing is everything, and He doesn't want to see you jealous of other people's blessings.

Do not question Him or doubt Him. That just insults our precious father. Have faith and trust that the Lord does not and will not forget you.

Psalm 94:14 proclaims, "For the Lord will not reject his people; He will never forsake His inheritance."

If you feel abandoned, remember that it is impossible for God to leave you, therefore you will never be abandoned. When you feel like He left you lonesome with your troubles, my precious advice is to calm down and don't move.

Be still.

He's there.

Day 29: Tight rope

If you've ever been to a circus then you most likely have seen the tight rope and maybe even watched someone perform on it, doing amazing tricks. It is so intriguing to watch someone walk across it and barely wobble, sometimes doing flips and cool acts on it. I can't even fathom the practice it takes to accomplish a skill like that, let alone even walk it without falling.

Imagine having to walk across the tight rope without practicing. We would most definitely wobble at the minimum. You would be unstable, unlike the people who have been rehearsed for years with hardcore practice.

Have you ever felt that in life you are walking along a tightrope for the first time, not knowing what you are doing, scared and ready to fall at any given moment?

I have, and it's horrible constantly feeling that way, unstable with decisions you have to make, ready to just fall.

A lot of the times, this is because we are not stable in our lives with certain aspects such as relationships, work, substance abuse, children, health problems, anxiety, anger issues, depression, and so on. We are leaning on our own understanding of everything, so we just walk as if we're on a tight rope. We could fix this problem by practicing.

Practicing would consist of reading the Word of God and asking him for direction and strength through these issues in our messy lives. You need a firm foundation, so you don't have to feel like you are going to fall at any given moment and constantly wobble.

You don't want to, and you don't need to feel that way all the time, like you need to grab a hold of anything you see and hang on for dear life.

Don't hang by a thread. The Lord says to call upon Him during times of trouble and to be anxious about nothing. We can rehearse this walk of life, and it doesn't have to be scary and wobbly. We can be strong and stand firm in the faith we have in God to help us through, so we can gloriously stride confidently along the tight rope we associate with life.

Rehearse your walk on the tight rope by following Christ and obeying His Word, that way you can perform, act, and stride across with confidence from the strength he gives you.

1 Corinthians 16:13 tells us, "Be on your guard; stand firm in the faith; be courageous; be strong."

Be steady, and be alert. There may be temptation headed your way persistent on making you fall, but you don't have to be anxious because trusting in the Lord will help you walk through these enemies.

Be confident and trust the Lord to hold your hand on this tight rope.

Day 30: Well Done

Remember as a child when you couldn't wait until you heard your parents say "well done" or "good job" to you when you finished a project nicely? Or maybe you appreciated it when your coach in school said, "awesome job," or it made you happy when your teacher told you that you wrote an awesome paper?

I remember very well on a few different occasions, even at a young age, hearing the words of "well done" and how it impacted me.

I have two older siblings so I am the baby. When I was younger, you can imagine I wanted to do everything they did. Their eyes would basically roll right out of their heads when I'd do this. I would always get jealous and upset if my parents asked them to do something but not me because I was "too young."

The result of that was me doing dishes on a stool at five years old or younger because I wanted to prove I could do what they could. It's still a joke in my family.

First of all, what five-year-old wants to do dishes that bad? I guess a five-year-old with jealousy. If you ask me, it's quite odd, but since I was the five-year-old I can say that. I am sure I didn't do the best job, and they had to rewash a lot of them, but they let me do them anyway. I'm sure my siblings were happy because they despised chores, especially dishes.

A lot of the reason I wanted to do them was because I wanted to be like my brother and sister, but also to hear my parents say, "good job" or "well done."

There are many occasions in life when we hear those words: maybe at our job, in a sports game, or just from family and friends. However, we must put in perspective who we really want to hear "well done" from.

Are we living for this world and wanting to serve it and make them happy? Or, are we living for God and looking for His loving words of "well done"?

God is the ultimate One we want to serve and glorify, which is why we must stop and think: are we doing something for man, or are we trying to please God?

In the end, it doesn't matter what the rest of the world thinks of us because we should want to please God and show Him how much we love Him rather than the world who fails us regularly. **Live to hear the Lord tell you "well done" not the rest of the world. They don't have a plan for you like He does.**

As Mathew 25:23 says, "His master replied, 'Well done, good and faithful servant! You have been faithful with a few things; I will put you in charge of many things. Come and share your master's happiness!"

Don't live life trying to please the world with what they want and want to hear. They can't give you true happiness, peace, or eternal life—only God can.

Look for a "well done" from the Lord and be faithful to Him, and you will share His happiness.

Day 31: Whose Time Are You On?

Don't you hate when you are waiting for food to be done in the oven and you just want to rush it, but you know it won't be as good? Or when something is in the microwave and you just stare at the time, thinking that will somehow make it go faster?

Maybe you are finishing an assignment for work or school, but don't have much time left, so you rush to get it done and its finished result is less than ideal.

It's a known fact that if we rush things, they usually don't come out as good as they would have if we waited in the first place.

I regularly get impatient and try to rush to get things done or push myself to beat a goal I had for a certain deadline. A lot of the times I'm left with results I don't like because I didn't wait for the right time.

We need to trust God's timing, rather than rush everything. If we don't go on his timing, then whatever we're pursuing will not be as good as what He plans.

If we rush God and do things on our own time, we are going to get that not-so-good microwave food rather than God's freshly baked goods.

Our timing is not always right because we tend to get impatient and rush, or we pick the wrong time for a lot of things because we don't know everything like the Lord does. God's timing is always perfect, and we need

97

to rely on that, not our own understanding.

As Ecclesiastes 8:6 proclaims, "For there is a proper time and procedure for every matter, though a person may be weighed down by misery."

Ask yourself whose time you're on. Are you on your time, or are you waiting on God's perfect timing where He has plans for you to prosper. Don't settle for microwave time, wait for the oven.

Think of your rushed timing as quick two-minute dinners or fast food, and think of the Lord's timing like waiting for a table at a renowned five-star restaurant. It's worth the wait!

Day 32: Trust Fall

In sixth grade my best friend and I did a lip sync to the song "Clumsy", and we choreographed the dance as well by ourselves (you can only imagine how that went).

It was cute when we did it then, of course, though when we hear this song now, our friends laugh and we question what we were thinking.

We were both so nervous to do that dance in front of the whole school back then, as well as family and friends. I was less nervous than my friend. I think she was honestly about to pass out, which made me start questioning how it was going to go.

At the last minute she wanted to back out. This made me nervous because there was a trust fall in the middle of the dance, which we made into a dance move, and she was the one who had to catch me.

I thought throughout the whole dance she was going to back out and run off the stage, which would leave me alone, unable to do that dance moves. Even though she did end up being there for me, I had fear during the entire dance that she would leave me alone.

We are so blessed to have a God that never backs out. We never have to have doubt or fear during these trust falls in our life because He doesn't hesitate.

He will always be behind us, ready to catch us. Sometimes catching us may be in the form of giving us strength to get through a situation If we fall because we disobey Him then He may catch you in a different form, such as showing His strength or showing us how much we really do need Him. He won't let us fall and leave us there. He loves us.

The Lord knows your heart, He knows your intentions, and He knows what you can handle. Don't be afraid that He will leave you because He is there ready to catch you when you fall, no matter what form He does it in. You can enjoy dancing, living your life, and praising God, because you don't have to question whether He will be there for you or not.

You can have complete faith that He will. God will not back out at the last minute. He promises to always be there, ready to catch you.

For Psalm 31:14 says, "But I trust in you, Lord; I say, 'You are my God.'"

He is our God, our father, and our protector—have comfort in Him. He wants our full trust, and He can show us the purpose He has for us and why we were created. He has a special, unique plan for us and will always catch us when we fall.

Keep repeating this to yourself.: He is your God. He is behind you at all times, ready for a trust fall while we are in this world where things can go wrong.

Day 33: He Knows

When you were growing up, did your mother or father ever say to you that they know you better than you know yourself? For instance, maybe you declined something they thought you'd need or want, such as a snack for school or a couple of water bottles for a sports game. Maybe they'd give it to you anyway because they knew you'd change your mind and end up wanting whatever it was.

A typical example would also be when you think you know what you want in life early on, like how many kids you want, when you want to have kids, what job you want, and the husband or wife that you want to spend the rest of your life with. You think you know.

We don't expect it, but sometimes those plans change. Like our parents, except more so, God knows our true hearts' desires. He knows us far better than we know ourselves. For example, that job you thought you wanted, God knew even before you were born that you'd hate it within three months. Or the man you thought you would spend the rest of your life with, God knew he wasn't for you. That's why He said no and closed that door.

God knows us better than we know ourselves, always and He is constantly watching out for us. You were created excellently and on purpose by the Creator of the universe, so of course He knows your true heart's desires.

Romans 8:27-28 explains, "And he who searches our hearts knows the mind of the Spirit, because the Spirit intercedes for God's people in accordance with the will of God. And we know that in all things God works for the good of those who love him, who have been called according to his purpose."

When we really want something, and God takes it away, we get mad and blame Him. Some of us curse and scream at Him, which I may be a possible culprit of, I'm not proud to admit.

This is because it's hard to understand that He knows in a few years if something won't work out, or that we won't like the job we're pursuing, which is why He says no and brings you somewhere else. He is protecting you.

If He says no, it's for a reason because He has our best interest. He's not doing it randomly or to be mean.

Have peace in knowing the Lord sees your life as a whole picture. He dipped his brushes in glory and painted your victory.

He knows.

Day 34: Remove and Resist

Don't you despise it when you get bit by mosquitoes and the bites on your skin are unbearably itchy?

When there are more than a few bites in different spots, it can make your whole body feel so horribly itchy. Your only desire in that time is to scratch yourself for hours on end. You know it will only make matters worse if you go ahead and cave in, scratching yourself until you feel the slightest bit better, but in the moment, you don't care because you're already itchy.

However, when we cave in and scratch ourselves especially too much, sometimes our skin is left being punctured which makes matters even worse than before.

This leads to my question of why don't we just remove the opportunity for this to happen in the first place? If we simply put on bug spray properly and remove the opportunity to get bit by mosquitoes and feel itchy the rest of the day or night, we wouldn't find ourselves having trouble with resisting the urge to scratch and make it worse.

If we just removed the opportunity for mosquitoes to bite, it also removes the opportunity for us to be tempted.

You know your weaknesses. You may try to hide from them or pretend they are not there, but sooner or later, you'll find yourself face to face with them.

Being tempted is part of being human, so don't feel abnormal for being tempted into something every day; it's something we all deal with.

You always will be tempted; you can't escape it. Since there is no possible way to avoid such nuisances, we can, however, avoid the opportunity from the beginning.

When I say avoid the opportunity, what I really mean is let these weaknesses and temptations that come our way, such as sexual desires, overeating, stealing, gossiping, guilt and shame, and maybe even shopping too much, cease.

Let them end before they start. Do not let your temptations even have the opportunity come near you or into your mind. For an example, if you have a drinking problem, you should never put yourself near alcohol, in a bar or around people who promote it. Why? Because it's an opportunity for you to cave.

As soon as you put yourself in the position to give into your greatest weakness, the temptations that reside there are ready to trick you more than ever. Let the opportunity cease and resist the urge for fake happiness.

If you find yourself surrounded by mosquitoes becoming their victim and being bit, resist the urge to scratch. You need to resist the temptation that latches on to you.

What/who are the mosquitoes in your life biting you and bringing you closer to your weaknesses? Maybe you would find God in being the bug spray in your life that protects you from these opportunities (except God works for everyone and bug spray may not).

Don't forget to use it and protect yourself. If you do get bit, it's crucial to resist and put on the itch cream, which you may compare to the word of God.

Move on from the temptations that want you so badly to scratch and scratch and scratch until you've fallen far from God.

It's perfectly easy to say and it's perfectly hard to do, but you can and you will once you keep doing it. You can resist. You know you don't want to feel the guilt and shame that comes after you give into your weaknesses where you ponder, inquire, and even query yourself all hours of the day as to why you would let yourself fall and be launched back to the beginning where new opportunities of attacks rise.

Wouldn't you rather feel victorious from conquering the urge and resisting the scratch? I know you would!

The Lord tells us many times to watch who we hang around because our company can corrupt us if they're not in the word. If anyone you surround yourself with is corrupting you and bringing you to situations that make you sin over and over again as well as cave into your weaknesses, there's one simple solution.

Re-evaluate who you are spending time with the most. Ask yourself if they are friends and co-workers who bring the best out of you or if they are people who respect your decision in resisting the urge from temptations that make you fall short from the glory of God.

If you take a look at Mathew 4:1-11. It shows a perfect example of how even Jesus, the Son of God was tempted by the devil. Over and over again, Satan tried to get Jesus to give in and be weak. The devil thought he had power over Jesus and that he could get Him to do anything. He was even quite tricky, but Jesus had God's favor and God's word.

As Jesus was in the wilderness alone where Satan decided to tempt Him, He refused the situation and didn't give in; since He knew God's word so well, He was able to resist and not hesitate.

He knew how God tells us not to test Him and to never worship any other gods and He stood by those commandments. The devil was unable to make Jesus fall through his tricks and temptations because Jesus resisted the urge.

He removed the opportunity quite sternly which is shown in Mathew 4:10-11: "Jesus said to him, 'Away from me, Satan! For it is written: Worship the Lord your God, and serve Him only.' Then the devil left him, and angels came and attended him."

Read the word and really study it. Know it in your heart, for when your temptations come around—which they will because remember we can never avoid them—know what the Lord says.

Know that He is your God, your protector, your friend and your Father who stands by you in your weakest moments.

Please resist the urge and don't give into false happiness that is fleeting. The serpent may be by your side trying every minute of the day, every day of the week, and every week of the year to trick you into doubting God and giving in, but God's power is more than that. So lean on Him, and trust He will walk you through.

When you remove the opportunity to be tempted into your weaknesses and choose to believe in the hope and trust you have in God to sustain you forever, resisting will become much easier.

My last bit of advice to you right now, is to spray the bug spray properly and evaluate who your company is. Identify the persuasions your surroundings have on you; remove yourself from places and people the Lord wouldn't categorize as ideal. Make sure you stick with it and resist every urge of sinful pleasures the world gives you that comes near, so you don't fall short. You will not have guilt and shame from resisting your weaknesses, but you will have blessings from obedience. Be patient, resist, and remove.

Remove all opportunities in your life that push you away from God and resist the urges the world gives you that display themselves as nothing but happiness, but are actually tricks from the devil. You can do this, and once you do it becomes easier, you'll feel amazing peace and joy from the Lord and you'll feel his true love that will sustain you.

Trust in the strength that the Lord provides you. Remove and resist temptations.

Day 35: Got Plans

Don't you just hate when you make plans and arrange your schedule, then all of the sudden those plans change out of the blue?

I can't stand that, but I'm also impatient with planning. I do understand, however, that things come up and life happens, but when it's just irresponsible or inconsiderate, I get so irritated. When I was in England studying abroad at Oxford, I went a day early to settle in and become at least a little familiar with my surroundings. I thought I was going to meet up with a friend I had made previously, so that I wasn't so alone, and their familiar face would make me feel better and more at home.

I was excited and felt more at ease knowing I would at least see this friend, since I didn't know anyone else in this unfamiliar country. As I got there I became all settled in, then took a few hours to venture downtown and see the city.

I was waiting to hear from my friend during this time, and after I went into the city and got back to my room, my friend gave me the heartbreaking news that they were not coming that day after all. You can imagine the disappointment.

What was I supposed to do? Just sit in my hotel room, sulking and feeling even more homesick? I felt even worse after that and was especially irritated. I hate when you wait for someone and they don't show up.

I couldn't believe the plan we agreed on changed at the last minute, since it was planned months ahead of time. The friendship ended up not working out for the better, and I realized that God changed the plans in order to protect me in continuing a friendship not meant for me.

I was mad and didn't understand at the time, but I now know and am grateful He was looking out for me. It took me a while to understand because I was upset it happened the first day I arrived abroad, but praise God for doing so.

We can make plans all we want, but we must be prepared that if they are not from God, they may change whether we like it or not. It's not in our control, and it never will be.

One of my favorite things to say is, "We make plans and God laughs."

He knows the good work He has planned out for us as well as the journey that is set ahead.

Our plans don't last, but God's do.

It's important to always ask God for His will and for Him to bring us in His direction, because His plans are the best while ours often fail.

You may be feeling upset right now because of something you planned ahead of time for several weeks, months—or worse—years. I get it, and I sympathize, but know that our plans are not the best plans, which is why we should never take our own path and always search for his.

I know that it's heartbreaking and disappointing when your plans fall through, especially when you were planning your schedule or life around them.

I've been there many, many times, but I've also been where the Lord chose for me to go instead of where I thought I was supposed to go. There is hope in that.

Proverbs 16:1 says, "To humans belong the plans of the heart, but from the Lord comes the proper answer of the tongues."

There will be times when God says "yes" to our plans and there will be times when he says, "not yet," delaying what we want, which makes us angry because we are impatient and lack understanding.

Then the Lord will tell us no because He has something far beyond what we can imagine. Something so much better.

Jeremiah 1:5 "Before I formed you in the womb I knew you, before you were born I set you apart; I appointed you as a prophet to the nations."

It's difficult when plans change, and you have to go out of your comfort zone. It is discouraging and quite upsetting, but have peace in knowing before you were born your future was planned.

Something to always remember is seen in Matthew 6:34 as it wisely says, "Therefore do not worry about tomorrow, for tomorrow will worry about itself. Each day has enough trouble of its own."

Day 36: Remember the Remedy

Think back on the times you were desperate for homemade remedies when you didn't feel good, or maybe you were trying to make a natural beauty product.

When you are sick, and it is your last resort, or when you are trying to make a face mask or coconut oil mixture for your hair, we nickname these things homemade remedies.

We try out anything in our homes as a last resort in hope that it will just maybe work for us.

When I was sick as a kid and felt nauseous, whether it was from a virus, from a long car ride, or a funny feeling, I couldn't stand it more than anything. I was and am the biggest baby when it comes to nausea.

Now, of course, I still can't stand it. I'm a bit much when it comes to that, especially because there is nothing you can usually do about it, since most of the time it just goes away on its own. As there are some medications to supposedly help, most of them do not work for me, which is why I would look up online natural remedies I haven't tried before to treat it.

I would rather have a constant cold for an entire year than be nauseous for a day—that shows how much I can't handle it.

Yes, you read that right, I'd rather live 365 days with a cold instead of being nauseous for one day. I find it to be the most repulsive feeling as it hinders me from doing anything the whole day.

This is why I would spend hours looking up homemade remedies online, in books, and asking around to effectively and immediately get rid of the nausea I felt.

I was desperate for homemade remedies because there was nothing else I could do, and it was my last resort. I would never find anything that worked or was safe to try that wasn't over the counter, since I had already tried many of them and they didn't work well for me.

As for beauty products, I would find some that were not too bad, but most would not work or have a long-lasting effect. However, the two had something in common. I did this for the slightest hope in feeling better or in the case of beauty, doing better. Now that I have you thinking about homemade remedies, there is one homemade remedy I stumbled upon that always works and is safe.

We have gone over it before and we have definitely all heard of it before, but maybe now you can look at it in a different way. This remedy is called trust.

Trust is the remedy made by God for our worries and anxiety, plus our doubt and sadness. Trust was created for us to follow by faith, which means not by sight, but belief.

The Lord created this so we can be comforted and not dwell in our sadness or search in the wrong areas for answers.

We have found a natural homemade remedy to our unfortunate sicknesses of anxiety and worries, made by God.

If we trust in Him and put all our worries and problems such as pain, doubt, guilt, and grief on Him, this

homemade remedy gives us peace.

The God of this universe gave His One and only Son to die for us, so the least we could do is trust in Him and use this homemade remedy from Him.

Trusting in the Lord, plain and simple, is the remedy to all struggles we face in life. There is nothing else in the world that can truly satisfy you and give you peace.

When you start to overthink and feel overwhelmed with stress and anxiety, remember this remedy you can use.

Do as the Lord says and put all your worries on Him when it is beyond your control, because it is in His hands. You cannot handle what happens out of your control; only our Savior can.

John 14:27 tells us we can have peace. We are told, "Peace I leave with you; my peace I give you. I do not give to you as the world gives. Do not let your hearts be troubled and do not be afraid."

There is no need for fear, because the Lord holds our hearts, our hands, and our world. Do not doubt Him and let your heart be troubled. The world cannot give you trust, because it disappoints you, unlike God. You may never understand why He does the things he does, but I pray you have peace knowing that He's aware of what you are going through, and your pain is not wasted.

He provided you with an amazing, all natural, homemade remedy. All you have to do is trust Him completely.

Your life is specially planned out by the Architect of everything, so be hopeful in the trust you can have. Use this remedy of trusting God that you are given, for anxiety, anger, sadness, hopelessness, sickness, brokenness, and heartache. Hand over your problems to the Author of true love and remember the remedy.

Day 37: GPS

Do you ever wonder what you would do without your map or GPS?

I often wonder what I'd do without my GPS, mostly because if I had to use a real map while driving, I would be lost for hours, not to mention extremely irritated.

I think for most people in this day and age, it is so easy and common to pull out your GPS when looking to get somewhere you have never before been. It doesn't take much effort.

My generation didn't grow up using maps. What would we do if we were lost in our car without any of these navigational technologies we so are used to and only had a map? Would we be able to get where we need to go?

What would we do without God as our remarkable life GPS? We sure don't know where we are going, and there are no certain maps to tell us our next step, which a lot of the time is terrifying. In life, we are lost without God, going in the wrong direction, not knowing where the next turn is, running stop signs and obvious red lights.

If we don't have a GPS, a map, or directions and we are going somewhere we've never been before, how would we get there? We wouldn't.

Turning around would be going backward, but if you go further you may be in an even worse situation and get even more lost.

Think of God as your GPS in life. He knows where to bring you. He knows your next turn, the next stop sign, and the next detour, so follow his way.

Whether it is declining a job, or that you're in the wrong relationship, or you're enabling your child, the Lord knows where all the stop signs should be and where they are.

Trust Him because He created the road and all the turns and road signs involved. You won't get lost if you believe, trust, and obey God.

Psalm 25:10 says, "All the ways of the Lord are loving and faithful toward those who keep the demands of his covenant."

Unlike the GPS we might use in our cars or on our cell phones, the Lord will never accidentally bring us in the wrong direction or stop working. He will always know where to go, even when they look like brand new roads and unseen paths to us.

When you go down a road you're unfamiliar with and you're feeling stressed, just remember that you need to be patient and go where the Lord tells you to.

Have hope in the fact that God will give you strength and always tell you when you need to stop, take a left, take a right or go straight.

Trust in Him, for He knows all the ways and will direct you.

Day 38: Lean

I've never driven a motorcycle before, but I have ridden on the back of one. I remember the first time was a lot different than I thought it would be.

I'll admit that it was fun, still very unfamiliar, which made it seem scary. If you drive a motorcycle or if you ride on them often, you will know that you have to be in control when you're the driver and make sure the person on the back is in sync with you.

When I say in sync, I mean that they need to be prepared to lean when going around a corner so it's smooth. If they do not lean, you both might fall. No one likes to tumble; it's not fun. It hurts and in some cases, it's a long recovery.

In life, if we do not lean with God when He leans, and we are not in sync during our ride with Him, we will fall, taking a hard tumble.

We have to lean when the Lord takes a turn, even if we can't see in front of us. We need to trust that He sees what's ahead and lean with Him when He turns.

He knows us better than we know ourselves. He sees the entire picture of our lives, before we were born and when we're with Him.

Psalm 37:24, "Though he stumble, he will not fall, for the LORD upholds him with his hand."

When you go on this ride with God, make sure you're in

117

sync with him and lean when He takes a turn. You don't want to fall, but you don't have to be scared either. Don't fear, for He can see the entire road ahead when you cannot. The Lord has you in complete care.

Day 39: Waves

I'm not going to sit here and pretend that life is so amazing and great all the time. I know it's not. However, I do believe life is amazing and great overall, despite its ups and downs, if you make it out to be.

Life is filled with blessings, overcomings, and waves of adversity as well as misfortunes, which is why we need to have a relationship with God when we are not only at peace, but shaken. Sometimes there are moments when you feel there is nothing you can do but lie in your bed for days and cry. Or, maybe other times you just want to sit and scream your head off—literally scream until anything, absolutely anything, gets better than what you are dealing with in that very moment.

If you were me, you would do all of what I just mentioned when feeling shaken. Having a relationship with God can help us feel more at peace when we go through trials and tribulations, so we don't have to scream and cry for days. I cannot imagine going through life and all its ups and downs without God.

Without God we have no hope. It sounds horrible to say we have no hope without him, but it's not because each and every one of us, not just a few select people are able to have a relationship with him and have amazing hope.

He is always there waiting for us to be with Him. He is our protector. He is our ultimate hero. He holds our hope in His mighty hands.

The Unfinished Puzzle

Ashley Alice White

I remember going to the beach when I was younger with my family a lot when we lived in Massachusetts. I remember my dad would always take me in the ocean while the rest of my family would lay on the beach or sometimes come into the water with us. I love the beach so I always wanted to be there but I was too young to go into the water alone.

To get off track for a moment, try and remember when you were young and you thought the waves were so scary and were going to harm you. My dad knew he wasn't going to let go of me in the water or that anything bad would happen to me because he was the one holding me knowing he would protect me. He wasn't going to let me go.

While I was helpless and weak, considering I was young lacking muscle and unable to touch the sand, I was frightened because I didn't realize how big the waves were or thought I would see sharks. I was crying and upset because I was scared and knew I couldn't touch the bottom. I don't think I realized what it would actually be like since I was playing in the sand always watching the waves and had a different perception. I knew if he let go, I would have no hope. I'd be hopeless in the water.

I had to trust my father and know that he would hold onto me and protect me. I had to give my full trust in him that he would get me out of the water safely because I was young and couldn't swim.

Just like I had to trust my father bringing me in the ocean, we need to trust God, our ultimate Father, in the troubling seas we catch ourselves in.

God knows there are big waves ahead of us, all around us, and even within us, but He promises to never let us go.

He knows the trouble that is ahead of us and He knows we can't handle it on our own.

With God, we are always safe, even in the waves of adversity, misfortunes and tribulations that crash in on us.

God is bigger than all of your problems. Be patient and you will see, He will pull you out of the water.

As Isaiah 41:10 proclaims, "So do not fear, for I am with you; do not be dismayed, for I am your God. I will strengthen you and help you; I will uphold you with my righteous right hand."

Nothing and no one can drag you down when you have God. We are all in his hands being upheld. He is our God, so we don't have to fear swimming through these waters. When you feel you can't touch the sand, know that the Lord has your back.

Day 40: Descend

This is one of my favorite things to write about, especially now because we are getting rid of these next few feelings addressed. We are not playing games. No games at all.

However, I shall warn you because these few words are not hopeful or happy, but what we are learning and going to do with them will be. They need to be addressed, confronted, and uninvited, especially since you are in your final descend, so close to arrival.

We will be getting rid of these words from your vocabulary, effective immediately. You will be telling, not asking for them to exit the way they entered.

These words are the devil's most potent words to use in order to interrupt your life in which they steal, destroy, and kill just like him. But no need to be afraid, because we have hope and we have trust, remember? The Lord is bigger than anything you face; He is your shield.

Doubt and worry.

The two depressing, drowning words that stop people from living a hopeful life are doubt and worry, which brings a load of anxiety and sadness.

Try not to let your heart stay wide open. What happens if you don't lock it? Of course, anyone can come in, and you know very well thieves will.

They're looking for the most precious jewels and riches in the world. God gives us these riches and divine jewels that we call hope, joy, love, and peace. When the door is not locked and shut only for God, there is a thief waiting at the doorstep to bust on in: the devil.

We definitely don't have time to play games with any thieves trying to steal our comfort the Lord brings us. Remember, if you don't lock it just for God, the devil will in fact jump in, replacing your finest jewels with little pebbles such as doubt and worry.

You have much hope with your heart because this is preventable. You can lock the door to your heart so that you can enjoy the abundance of blessings the Lord gives you.

God has a key to your heart as soon as you ask Him to enter. He will never leave; He will live there forever. However, He should be the only one with this key so that intruders do not break in. When He has the key to our hearts, He will help determine who else is allowed in. Ask the Lord to enter your heart. Do it now. He's waiting. He wants to be with you forever and He's waiting to prosper you; don't waste your time on the lies of the devil.

Let's take the time to uninvite doubt and worry. Tell them to exit. Throughout your day, do not let anyone else into your heart if they are not from God. Remember to lock your door so you can enjoy the Lord's blessings. You are now in your final descent to your final destination: hope. This is where you will be uninviting many things that keep you from victory with the Lord.

As we start our descent, please prepare for landing phase.

Day 41: Lock Your Doors

My brother, sister, and I would always watch the movie *Dennis The Menace* and laugh at the thief in it because he would do silly things that made us laugh when we were young. We would call him "The Dirty Guy" even though that was not his name, or even his character's name.

Even now, years and years later we will still bring him up and use that terminology. It was just something we would laugh at because he was filthy in the movie with dirt all over him. He would steal any chance he got.

He'd say, "I bet they don't even lock their doors," referring to the people in the town.

To add onto the concept of locking our doors as briefly mentioned in your final descent, let's dive into it a little deeper now. This is exactly what the devil says about us! He loves to break and enter into our hearts, and once he gets in, it's very easy for him to steal. We have to make sure we lock our doors and let no strangers in.

We cannot afford the devil to steal our joy. He opens the door to our hearts when they're wide open and takes our joy—he snatches it! When he takes our joy, it is replaced with worry and fear. To him, he becomes a rich man, because he feels he is stealing from the Lord, just like a thief becomes rich from all the jewels and money they steal from homes and people.

We cannot let the devil in. We need to lock our doors at all times! The Lord has blessed you and intends for you to be joyous about his blessings. Do not let anyone steal your joy!

This next verse I am going to introduce to you is important, so please read it carefully. I want you to remember it.

John 10:10 says, "The thief comes only to steal and kill and destroy; I have come that they may have life, and have it to the full."

God's Word warns us of the thief. He will steal if he can't kill, and he will do anything in his power to destroy us. He may use people even if they don't know what they are doing to destroy you and your relationships, especially your relationship with God.

The devil can't stand God getting glory, so he will do anything in his power to attack you so that you give up. The Lord has so much more power than him, so fear not. But you still need to lock the door to your heart. **Do not let anyone steal your joy the Lord has blessed you with. The Lord intended it for you, only.**

So go ahead, uninvite the thieves who are stealing your joy.

Day 42: Who Says We're Not Good Enough?

There have been countless times that someone has made me feel not good enough, not skinny enough, not pretty enough, not smart enough, and the list goes on...

I am sure most of you in your lifetime have felt this way one time or another, which only means you can relate to this.

Isn't it just the worst feeling when you are broken up with or you don't get the job you wanted, because in your mind it means you are not good enough? Even worse, you don't get into the college you wanted, or maybe none at all?

It feels awful.

I can't shake the feeling of getting rejected when these things happen. I'm the culprit of dwelling upon it. I think there is just no other feeling that makes you feel lower than when someone tells you that you're not good enough or makes you feel that way anyway.

This is why I don't like the word "less." Less is an awful word because it means not enough in most situations.

Instead of feeling like "less," you should look on the bright side of things.

I know you won't feel like looking on the bright side when bad things happen, which is why we need to have a good relationship with God because He is the bright side.

God has something better when people tell us no or that we are not enough.

If someone you're dating dumps you, realize God is showing you He has someone better for you. **The Lord decides and says, "No, this is not for you, I have something better, I have something else."**

Take the time to learn about why people are telling you no and making you possibly feel not good enough. For starters, know that sometimes it could be the devil trying to tear you down and turn from God when you're getting close to him. He is known specifically for doing that, and it's the one thing he is good at, but it never overrides the Lord's power.

Rejoice in the fact that God is picking you out, specifically, to do something else, to be with someone else. He has a perfect plan set out for you. You are not less than anything or anyone.

Start each morning by proclaiming that, because it's true. There is no single person on this earth that you are less than. We are only less than the Almighty Father, who tells us we are enough, always.

I know it's extremely hard when you're already in a bad mood about the situation you're in and feeling down and not enough, but please remember the Lord thinks highly of you, and He sent his Son to die for you.

The word "less" should never enter your mind when you're thinking of yourself. You are less than no one, but please be careful with knowing that because you are also not higher than anyone.

Did you read that correctly? The Lord loves you. YOU! He says you are good enough, even better, that you are more than enough. "More than enough" is what you should repeat to yourself. He loves you so much that He washes away your sins to give you eternal life.

Do not feel down today about any of the people or things that make you feel like that awful word described above.

You might be reading this and still think, "No way will God give me something better, because what I want is only what I want, and my way is the best way. If I don't get this, then I will never be satisfied."

But know this: the Lord will surprise you. Remember He is supernatural and knows you better than you know yourself. He says that what he has planned is far more than what we will ever dream. What you're dreaming, know that God has something much more than that, something much greater, if you follow His direction. He knows your mind and your heart, the true desires that are within you.

Don't let anyone make you feel that you are incapable and that you are not enough for them. Listen to ONLY what the Lord says. He says we are good enough. He made a divine plan for you in which He wants to see you succeed.

He specifically made you for a purpose, and that reason may not be revealed yet, which is why patience is required.

You most likely don't understand what you are going through and why, but the Lord does and He has a divine plan awaiting.

There is no such thing as all closed doors. There is always going to be another door opened with God. You are good enough, and you have hope to a better future.

When someone tells you no, understand that God is about to tell you yes to something greater.

2 Corinthians 3:5 says, "Not that we are competent in ourselves to claim anything for ourselves, but our competence comes from God."

We are sufficient, not on our own, but with God we can do all things; we are sufficient in Him.

Uninvite the word "less" because you don't need it anymore; you cannot accept it. Never let it near you again. Don't even let yourself hear it.

Today you are going to know and proclaim you're more than enough and that you are here right now, in this season for a purpose where the Lord will harvest you!

Day 43: He Felt It First

What is the reason you don't do certain things you'd love to do that you're passionate about? What makes your heart beat and pump for joy? What prevents you from not moving forward or taking a risk?

My excuse is fear. I bet a lot of you said that too. I find it to be one of the worst things to deal with. I can't stand it, so I avoid it.

I can't bear to have to even think of the rejection I will inevitably have to deal with in many aspects in my life. Writing about it makes me cringe even, as it's awful to think about, but will happen in our life.

Being rejected will happen to you, no matter what, for you cannot escape it. We are unable to avoid it. The feeling you feel, the sting you can't shake, the uncertainty you have that rejection so kindly brings forth—you're not alone in feeling it.

Believe it or not, Jesus was the king of rejection. He feels our pain. In fact, He felt it worse than we ever will. Feelings of betrayal and being rejected, Jesus felt it first. You will feel pain and heartache you can't get away from, but have peace in the fact that Jesus was there first before you and I.

He had people hate him, He had people slander and beat Him; He was first.

Whatever we are going through, we are not going through alone. We're never alone. Did you know that? Even if you did, you must be reminded of it.

The Lord's presence is all around us at all times. He is everywhere all the time. We are never left alone, which is so amazing because when we're physically alone and feel that our friends and family are not there, the Lord is by our sides.

Something I have always dealt with is being alone. I can't stand it.

I am so much happier with people around, especially with commotion. I just love being with people. When I am traveling alone, and I'm not around people I know, sometimes I get upset because I feel so isolated.

I like to share experiences with my friends and family. I had to learn to be okay with being by myself, and I was able to do that because I learned that the Lord will always be with me when my friends and family cannot be.

My forever friend is always there. He never leaves me, and He never leaves you.

This makes me feel so much better during times of fear and doubt. I know the Lord felt heartache first, and I know that He understands and will always be with me.

When I feel rejected, or I plain old do get rejected, I know He was rejected first and I know He will never reject me.

Maybe you feel like this is it for you, like no one actually loves you, or that you're worthless or you will never be good enough. It's awful to say, but it's true sometimes we feel that way. I know it seems as if I'm bringing up negative feelings, but hang in there for a bit. I'm here to share the best news with you.

You are quite the opposite of all that, remember who created you!

And that's not it, there's more!

As Jesus not only tells us that not only are we more than enough, he tells us to put our pain on Him. Do you see how much He loves us? He died not only for our sins, but so we can lean on Him during our times of heartache and suffering.

So do it, lean on Him. He felt your pain, He felt your rejection. He identifies with us. Lean on the Lord with all your troubles. He does not reject you. He is our Father, our ultimate hero. The one and only King of all Kings that can do all things, and He wants YOU to put your pain on Him. The Lord will always claim us as His children and never forsake us.

We are enough for Him, and don't ever forget it! Do not fear rejection, because when the world rejects you, the Lord does not.

He will close a door, but only for your protection. When he opens a door, there is no man who can shut it. Look at Revelation 3:7 which says, "To the angel of the church in Philadelphia write: These are the words of him who is holy and true, who holds the key of David. What he opens no one can shut, and what he shuts no one can open." This is a promise from Him.

Always remember this: "If the world hates you, keep in mind that it hated me first," which John 15:18 boldly says.

We were not the first to feel pain, therefore we can have peace in knowing we can survive it with our hero by our side. He was here first being slandered, beaten, hated, and rejected.

Really listen and understand what that Scriptures says. He knows and feels your pain. Have peace knowing that the Lord claims us, and while the world may reject us, we know he prepares a special seat at his home where we will be accepted. Don't fear anything, because what man cannot do, the Lord can.

He was beaten before us, He was slandered first, He was hated first, and He was betrayed first. Everything you and I feel now, He felt it first.

You're not alone in this matter and you have the most extraordinary gift where you can put all your pain and suffering on the Lord. He takes it in His hands and gives you peace. So lean on Him, do it now and receive the peace He wants to gift you.

So my advice to you is to uninvite rejection from your home. Your home is your heart where fear is not allowed, and rejection cannot visit. They're done and they over-stayed their welcome. Peace is here and joy is coming to stay with you forever. As you kick the old guests out, prepare to welcome the next two from the Lord.

Day 44: Can You Say "Grudge"?

Forgiving.

Oh my, this is a tough one. Don't lose me here. Some people are gifted in the way that they can forgive easy, but if you are like me, you are nowhere near gifted that way.

It's difficult and involves a lot that you may not necessarily deal with such as getting over yourself and moving on, which completely kicks you out of your comfort zone.

Sometimes I would think when I have to forgive someone and finally say that I forgive them, I felt as if I am swallowing my pride. I definitely didn't want to have to do that, no thanks. I would rather keep it where I am familiar and comfortable.

It's so easy to stay mad at someone for a while. I would always stay mad for so long even when sometimes I didn't want to, but I just couldn't bear to swallow my pride.

I would finally get the desire to forgive my friends or my family that I was mad at, but sometimes I just couldn't because of the stubbornness that took over and can even now still take over, considering it is a work in progress.

Even now I have a hard time with it. It's not an easy thing to do, especially when someone rips your heart right out with no warning at all.

I started thinking about how sad, disappointed, and heartbroken I can get when someone makes me angry.

Usually, right when someone makes you mad or offends you, you don't forgive them within seconds. It takes time, doesn't it?

It's not usually the case that when someone makes you so mad and immediately seconds after or even right when they do it, like a robot, you forgive them. It takes time even to process what happened and the emotions you feel before forgiveness crosses your mind with most people.

What if every day, multiple times a day, you had to forgive friends, family, co-workers, and everyone you know—no matter what the issue was, right when they wronged you, right when you felt heartbroken, and have to instantly genuinely forgive them?

Remember the feeling when someone makes you mad, and how hard it would be to instantly forgive them. To just let it go and move on, instantly without questions, or any time to think. That sounds quite difficult, doesn't it?

Maybe you're grinding your teeth even thinking about having to do that. For the stubborn people reading this, don't worry, I'm included. Could you even bear that? I feel like I wouldn't be capable of doing that, definitely not without God's strength.

However, there is someone who does that every day, all day, and all night—no matter what the damage is. He does it with love, grace, mercy, and compassion. God promises to forgive us of our sins when we repentant, always.

It doesn't matter how sad we make him with our disobedience, He will always and forever forgive us when we ask from our hearts and turn from that sin.

Without doing this, we break the fellowship we had with Him.

This doesn't mean we can keep doing what we do that brings God great displeasure over and over again just because He forgives. If we don't confess before Him and truly repent, asking for strength with our weaknesses, then true blessings from Him will not come your way. You separate yourself from God when you refuse to confess and turn from your sin.

However, here's the great news: When you believe in the Lord, truly and faithfully, you are forgiven right as you repent and diligently work on turning from your weaknesses.

This means that when you repent to God from the bottom of your heart, you're instantly forgiven, and your sins are forgotten. He knows your sin, as well as what you have done, but He does not think of it. You are not looked at as sinful, but as a new creation when He forgives.

His love does not change, no matter what you have done. Don't break your fellowship with God, because He forgives instantly, right when you repent, if you truly believe.

How amazing is that? We have a God so brilliant and gracious that when we repent and truly mean it, He is there to forgive and help strengthen us from our sins.

As God made us in His image, we must aspire to be like Him always in every aspect of our life. To every day strive and shed light. As God forgives, we should too.

Of course, it's harder for us to forgive, and sometimes there are things we just can't forgive, but we need to try and show the world the love, mercy and grace God is.

Not only is it obeying God to forgive those who have wronged you as well as yourself, it will make you more at peace as well as right with God. If we could be more like Christ and forgive like He does, there would be a lot more peace within you as well as others.

Although, if we keep the mindset of "God forgives, I don't," your heart will be hardened and cold. Your fellowship and relationship with the Lord will be broken.

Trust me, I know exactly how it feels to never want to forgive someone, or even to see them again in the moment of it all, but try right now just forgiving someone in your heart that has wronged you so badly that you can't even bear to say their name.

Forgive them and move on.

Your heart will become lighter, happier, more hopeful, and beautiful.

Forgive the unforgiven people in your heart. Make some room for peace, love, joy, and especially, the Lord.

You don't have time for a hard heart that holds grudges. Make some more room.

Show the light from the Lord as He forgives you, no matter what the damage was. Forgive more and make some room. Aspire to have peace, and shed love on those who have wronged you, after all we are not perfect either.

Forgiving doesn't mean you have to trust someone, but it means you are letting go of the darkness held in your heart.

Think of all the sadness we cause Jesus when we disobey time after time again. He still forgives us, loves us, and never forsakes us.

Even if you forgive one person in your heart, you will have so much more peace than you did before. Start by forgiving someone today, and remember to truly repent to the Lord and believe in His faithfulness and loyalty to you.

As Colossians 3:13 says, "Bear with each other and forgive one another if any of you has a grievance against someone. Forgive as the Lord forgave you."

Let go of those dark grudges. Don't let them cling to you—uninvite them.

Forgive as the Lord forgave you and repent before Him. Bow down to the Lord who died for you. He's here to forgive you and bring salvation.

Day 45: Last is First and First is Last

A lot of people in this world look at the acquisition of material things as the most important and highest goal to achieve. A lot of the time just the status of looking like the most prestigious, highly celebrated person from ownership of fancy material means is what people look for. To be the best is the most important thing to many, many people. To be on top, named chief, or be in high command, illustrates the mindset in their minds that those things mean they are number one.

Many people think being on top, having everything, and being rich are the most important things in life.

I've caught myself putting a lot of this on my back, and it made me miserable to become what I thought would make me the supposable best. This only resulted in an unhappy, tiresome phase of life.

I learned this most significantly while in Haiti in the village of Pavillon, and I now know none of those things make one happy.

As I finally reached the top of the mountain, after a few hours of driving and hiking through a rough stream, I saw a little girl standing in the muddy trail with a bottle of water. She was smiling at all of us but did not speak English. The lady I was with, who spoke both English and Creole, said the water was for me.

This little girl did not have much, but she waited patiently as I finally arrived to her village to hand me this bottled water, they were aware my father and I were from the States, meaning we couldn't have the water they drink.

This little girl took the time, happily and unselfishly, to climb down from the top of where the village she lived in to wait until she saw us and give me water. She couldn't wait to do this because she wanted to make me comfortable.

From this moment onward, I was blessed with being able to finally understand what it means to be rich. The Lord tells us that we are not rich from what we have, rather who we seek and give of ourselves in serving others. The poorest man in the world, who barely has anything, but is willing to still serve the Lord with a pure heart is considered the richest of all, because material things will always ruin, be out of date, and never keep us satisfied.

But the heart of man that belongs to God will prosper forever. To have many material things, many successes, titles and awards is great. Most people love those things, but once it starts to be the only thing you are focused on, true joy will never be experienced.

God gives us true joy that will never fade, unlike material riches we think we need to be happy. Know that those will be out of date and vanish quickly.

I witnessed people with nothing, absolutely nothing, smile and praise God. They were willing to help us with anything we needed, without a favor in return, helping us when not asked.

They didn't expect, they just simply had joy in wanting to take care of us and make sure we were happy and safe. These were people who don't have homes and struggle to eat every day of their lives.

This showed me how rich they really are in spirit because they are simply happy to help us, serving the Lord so faithfully. They were full of joy when they had nothing, while some people, even I, suffered from sadness even when I had everything.

I learned fully that the material things you want to chase won't make you rich or happy. Only satisfying yourself in the Lord is when you're richest of all, after all he always provides.

If you are the richest, most successful person on the planet, that is great and wonderful, but know that it does not make you the best person alive.

Material things will not get you inside the golden gates with the Lord.

Read this carefully, especially when you think you need to be the best.

When someone makes you feel unworthy and not important, when you are told you are not good enough and that you are not number one, remember that getting into heaven won't be chosen by who has the most money, or who has the most successes. So remember this verse.

Mathew 20:16 says, "So the last will be first, and the first will be last."

The little girl who gave me the water, when she needed it more than I did, may have been the richest young girl I have ever met. She was unselfish and full of love; she had real joy.

She was able to give away something she desperately needed to a person a lot more fortunate than her.

Through this time I was able to see Jesus because that was something He always did. She will not be last, she will be first.

As she doesn't have much money (if any), clothes, an education, and a steady home, she was still the richest of all.

You cannot buy your way into God's kingdom by stomping to the top with successes and coins. Your heart is what the Lord sees and what He wants. He wants your joy in serving Him and helping others.

I am so blessed to have experienced real love from someone so much younger and less fortunate than I, because I gained true joy that day and found what it means to be rich and joyful.

I experienced real love.

If you were feeling hopeless today and that you don't have a lot of material things the rest of the world has, or that someone else has a better education than you do, be encouraged that the Lord does not look at any of those things.

He looks at where your true heart lies, not where your wallet is or what your diploma says. The Lord will call you first, as you are never, ever last in His eyes when you display your beautiful unselfish heart.

If you are fortunate to have a lot of money, or you have a lot of extra things you know you don't need, that is amazing. A lot of people work very hard for these successes and great wealth. I have so much respect for that.

However, the Lord tells us in His word to share when we have great wealth, as He shared with many. This doesn't mean give up everything you own or put everyone else before your family. No, it just means share what you can and don't be selfish. The Lord does not like selfishness and won't accept it. You will not find true joy and blessings from God when acting selfish. Remember that 2 Corinthians 9:7 says, "Each of you should give what you have decided in your heart to give, not reluctantly or under compulsion, for God loves a cheerful giver." Be a cheerful giver rather than being reluctant and hesitant on sharing. Act in a way that you would want others to act towards you.

Encourage yourself to help out others today wherever you are. Do the best you can and never idolize success and material things that the world says you need.

For God has the final say in who is first and who is last. He will give you the most wondrous riches of all. He may bless you with great wealth, but don't idolize it or be selfish with it.

Luke 3:11 says, John answered "Anyone who has two shirts should share with the one who has none, and anyone who has food should do the same."

Uninvite the selfishness that Satan wants you so badly to have. Don't let it overcome you. Share as Jesus did. You will be greatly blessed for the selfless love you shed.

Day 46: Disappointment

For the first time in a long time, I felt like I was a young girl who was told she would get a puppy, then never did.

Disappointment.

My goodness, it's drowning. Getting your hopes up, thinking your dreams are almost reachable, then bam they're crushed, so easily.

There is nothing you can do about it either, because you're not going to settle. You can move on and look forward to what God has for you in the future and His better plans, but you'll still feel disappointment in the meantime.

As I am writing this, I am reflecting on how I felt earlier, and how disappointed I was. That cringe-worthy feeling of almost reaching, close to grabbing even, your dreams you thought you'd obtain.

I went to the doctor's office thinking I was going to leave with high hopes of feeling better and having a solution. I was told previously I had an auto immune disease as well as a nodule on my thyroid which they were investigating. I was excited because I thought they were going to give me medication to balance my levels or some kind of solution so I would feel remarkably better. As I talked to many people with the same condition, they gave me hope as well because they received medication and are doing a lot better. Then I was basically told at that moment there was nothing they could do for me.

I was crushed, and I held back tears, barely. Most of them

streamed down my face, but I held back the not-so-silent sobs I would have let out if I was a little girl still.

I thought I was going home with good news and would start feeling better soon. I was so hopeful. But I left with disappointment and the feeling of never wanting to hope again because of the slight risk of being disappointed again.

How do you really get over disappointment? It can be so bad that you let it ruin your entire day, which people often do. Again, I found something I need to work on.

Sometimes the only logical things that you think will make you feel better are to cry, sulk, dwell, pout, or take it out on other people. It is our initially reaction in most cases. Sometimes we react in ways we soon regret.

I understand that there are worse situations throughout the world than what I went through on this day, and even I have been in worse situations than that too.

I still, however, felt tremendously heartbroken and disappointed. It hurt and I was angry. I felt there was no way I could praise God through this. Why would I? He didn't give me what I wanted, and I have been abundantly obedient.

So I thought: *I'm done. I'm done going his way it gets me nowhere.*

Sometimes we go through these times. It's annoying, it's sad, and it's a huge inconvenience, but we have to go through it and push through until we're out in the clear. The only person who knows why we are disappointed and has the plan for the disappointment is God.

After this happened, I was overwhelmed with sadness because I didn't leave with what I wanted. As I said earlier, I felt like a child without a puppy when I was promised one.

I learned much after this time and what I wanted was not best for me at that moment. I had to trust God more and not fear for the outcome. It was a time for my faith to grow and my trust to be tested and strengthened.

The Lord saved me from me getting what I thought I wanted. As I so badly wanted an immediate solution to fix this disease I had. I learned that it would cause more problems at that moment because there were other underlying health issues needed to be fixed first. I prayed hard for medication to be the solution because I thought it was the best and easiest for me when it wasn't. After being explained more in detail on why medication would cause more problems, I realized that God was protecting me from an even bigger problem. I didn't see the entire picture so I thought I knew what I wanted when in reality I didn't. I was trying to force pieces of the puzzle to fit because I didn't see the whole picture. I needed to surrender my puzzle to God.

We will go through so many disappointments, and maybe not find out until hours, months, or even years later why. But there is always a reason for it.

Have peace in knowing that God will not waste your pain. He has a wonderful purpose for it, and you will see soon that it is used for good.

Psalm 34:18 says, "The Lord is close to the brokenhearted and saves those who are crushed in spirit."

God knows we are upset, disappointed, and brokenhearted, but He's always near us during these challenging times. He knows the next move and the next door to open that we can't see.

God wants us to draw near Him during these times, so we can lean on Him and be comforted by His love and peace.

He wants to make us stronger, to bless us abundantly, and to learn. Even though we can't see what great works He is doing, that doesn't mean it's not happening, even in the darkest situations that seem impossible, especially if you're told they are impossible.

I know being disappointed is awful and ruins your day. Sometimes it's so bad it debilitates you from doing anything, but don't let that happen. That is Satan creating a plan of attack against your faith in the Lord.

He hates when you're near God. He despises it and will do absolutely anything to pull you away from God.

Once he does that, his mission is complete. Draw very close to God when you're disappointed. You will need His strength to carry you until you've reached the victory the Lord set out for you.

Don't turn from God. He's not disappointing you, He is setting you up for something even better. He is using your pain for good and helping you become strong. Uninvite this feeling and open your heart to trusting the Lord.

Day 47: Only a Reflection

There was a time when I was slandered, and it broke my heart.

I had no idea for months that it was happening and this was because most of the things people heard about me, were uncomfortable things to talk about, therefore no one brought it up to me, until months later. I was so hurt and embarrassed, especially because they were disgusting, complete and elaborate lies made up about me from someone I thought was a friend.

The worst part about it was that I was studying abroad in Oxford most of the time this was happening, so I was unable to stop it, especially since I didn't know it was going on and I was out of the country while it happened in the states.

I was upset, confused, and overall very hurt.

The one thing that made me heartbroken about all of this was someone saying, "I thought she was supposed to be a strong Christian."

Of course, they were saying this because they heard rumors about me which they thought were true, so my behavior and character came into question, since I am a Christian. This really broke my heart because I had never had to deal with this before, also because it mocked something near and dear to my heart: my Christianity.

There was nothing I could have done about it. It was already said and done by the person who I thought was my friend, and it was probably said to people I don't even know about. As I told as many people as I could that it wasn't true, and most people came to see that, I also knew that it was impossible to know every single person she spoke to about me.

The one thing I could do is disengage from that environment and get out of that polluted toxicity that person brought. I had to trust that God would get me out of that water.

I had no idea why God was allowing this to happen to me. I was mad because I was obedient to Him, and He didn't stop this from happening. I didn't understand then that obedience has nothing to do with what happens to us a lot of the time, and that it was part of His plan for me. Everything that happens is a journey I am on with the Lord.

What I had to remember, which was hard to at the time, was that He sees the entire picture of my life and knows what I can and cannot handle as well as what is true and what is not.

He gives us trials many times to learn and strengthen our faith. Although I was unhappy and heartbroken about this situation, He strengthened my faith and showed me He will follow through.

I didn't have to understand what He was doing in that time of tribulation, but I did have to trust Him. Even though I was hurt and angry, even with Him, I had to trust that He was going to pull through on this.

This incident was taken care of, and I finally stuck up for myself with the strength God gave me. I learned how to value myself and how to lean on family and friends during that time. As I just turned my cheek and didn't seek out revenge on this person because I knew that would be wrong and hurtful, I saw that it was time to end the "friendship." I also saw how a lot of people stood up for me and were there for me during that time. It was beautiful to see how people come together and help each other.

The Lord showed me through this unfortunate event that I am so loved by so many friends and my family, and that He will always fulfill his promises to me.

I hope you are encouraged to know that God will fulfill His promises. So please, don't give up. God knows your heart and He knows the truth.

He will come through and replenish you with something good, something even better. He sees who is slandering you, and He sees you're being obedient and faithful. God has a plan for this time in your life, even if it's a season of pain.

It may hurt and feel awful when people think or say things about you that are not true, but the importance is that the Lord knows the truth and He will see you through it. He will be there for you in these times and bring you through the dark tunnel until you find the light.

The picture of your life is not revealed to you. You can only see a glimpse, but know that He sees the entire picture which is why He brings you through dark times in order to get you where you need to be.

During your times of pain and hurt—and especially confusion—on where the Lord is bringing you in your life, know that He will follow through. You may feel like you're sinking in the sand, but God won't let you, because He fully knows what you are capable of.

1 Corinthians 13:12 says, "For Now we see only a reflection as in a mirror; then we shall see face to face. Now I know in part; then I shall know fully, even as I am fully known."

You will soon see Him face-to-face. Be patient my friends, you will soon fully know. So, again, go ahead and tell these feelings of abandonment to leave and never return. Uninvite them, confront them face-to-face and refuse to feel it again, because you know you're not abandoned for the Lord is with you and soon you will see Him where victory is shown and pain is gone.

You're in temporary pain until victory is shown.

Day 48: Don't Turn To Salt

When was a time that someone told you not to turn around, or to never look back figuratively? Was it after a breakup, or moving away? Maybe you are graduating high school or college and you are moving onto graduate school.

I remember so many instances when I was told that, such as a time when I was young, playing soccer.

My coach would say, "Once you get the ball, just run with it and don't look back, or it will slow you down."

Another time I heard it was when I dated someone, and I needed to move forward and not look back after breaking up with them, and then there are just the mistakes I made and needed to move on from. I needed to move forward and to never look back, as it slows us down.

The Lord tells us that too. He says it quite clearly. What He means is don't look back to your past and your past mistakes. Everything you have done, don't look back and dwell on it, because He forgave us already.

He made you new. He doesn't look at your past now, and He won't in the future. Even though He knows us, and knows everything about us, He is not going to look at our past and judge us when we ask him for forgiveness. Certain things you may have done in the past may make you think: *There is no way God would love me, there is no way I can live a Christian life, and there is no way I can be a good person and change.*

The Unfinished Puzzle   Ashley Alice White

A lot of people think those things once they make a horrible mistake, like there is no way they can be forgiven by God, which I have done and sometimes do.

I have made many mistakes, and I know for a fact I will make more.

I have had people say to me and about me, "I thought you were a Christian" when I make a mistake, or I did or said something that God wouldn't care for.

But the untold truth comes again, because Christians make mistakes, always. We all do, Christian or not.

We don't like to and we don't always mean to, we definitely don't want to, but mistakes happen and always will happen since we are not perfect. We are all human and we are all going to do it because we fell short from the glory of God.

We are so blessed that our God does not look at our past and judge us upon that. Imagine if we could only enter heaven if He just said, "Let me see your resume; what have you done?"

None of us would enter those gates if we made too many awful mistakes. Actually, even just one small sin would disqualify us, which is why we should constantly thank the Lord for dying for our sins. Our sins can be erased if and only if we truly repent to our Father, the Lord and Savior. This ties into forgiving, when we talked about instant forgiveness—a quality the Lord has.

We should be so grateful to Him and praise Him for the forgiveness He gives us. Once we are forgiven, our past does not matter in God's eyes—it is over with and made new.

We should move with God and never look back, only better our future and keep going. Like my soccer coach

once told me, it only slows us down, so don't look back.

You are new, so start new, and live new. Don't look back and slow yourself down.

Genesis 19:26 says, "But Lot's wife looked back, and she became a pillar of salt."

There is a story that goes behind this verse. To shorten it significantly, the Lord told Lot's wife to not look back at Sodom when they were escaping the cities being destroyed. She was curious and wanted to, so she did; she gave into temptation. She disobeyed God and didn't trust Him when He told her not to ever look back.

She couldn't kill the curiosity she had because she was tempted, resulting in disobedience which cost her. Once she looked back, as God said not to, she turned into a pillar of salt. She didn't listen to a word He said, and it cost her greatly. We must learn from her mistakes and obey God, because when we look back, we fail to see the Lord.

If you look back, that just sticks you in your past, and you won't be able to move forward if you keep looking there. When God forgives you, you need to also forgive yourself and move on. You can't go into your future when you're always looking back and not turning away.

Don't become a pillar of salt. Keep looking forward so you don't slow yourself down. Uninvite the curiosity that will kill you, don't let temptation drag you down. Do not accept these into your mind. Read the Word of God, renew your mind, and think as He would want you to. Focus on Him. You will receive truth. So go ahead, uninvite.

Day 49: Washed Away

We can all be so quick to judge people when we don't know them, or even when we do know them, we do it anyway.

It's even worse when someone tells us wrong information and we judge upon that false information we receive. I have judged people countless times, and I am positive I have been judged countless times too.

The thought of me being judged by another person makes me uncomfortable because, well, who wants to be thought badly about? I certainly don't. I'd like to think that I live in a perfect place where everyone loves me and thinks only good things, but I know it's not true, and I have to accept that I don't live in a perfect place, especially when I'm nowhere near perfect.

How are we judged? For starters, sometimes people watch us from afar and see our actions, what we do and what we say.

Then, of course, people hear things that may be taken out of context or just not true, but generally people see our actions and judge us.

We as Christians are judged easily, and we're easy targets. I learned this the hard way. A lot of people judge us harder because they think we can't mess up or that we proclaim we don't.

We will mess up. We are human. We all mess up and we

make mistakes—daily, in fact.

We are not God. None of us are, but we should try our best every day to show an example of Him and His love He always sheds on us unconditionally.

The untold truth is if you mess up, and sometimes if you are a Christian and mess up, you will be judged harder because of the misconception people think you have to be or proclaim to be. You may even be slandered the way I was when I was abroad, hopefully not.

It's tough, and it hurts.

The point of me telling you this is to encourage you today to remember why Jesus died for us. Not all the time, but sometimes I have experienced people thinking that if you're a Christian then you have no room for mistakes, and you are fake if you make one. I don't know why that is thought, but it's happened to me multiple times. There is not one single person on this earth that is perfect. If someone becomes a Christian or is a Christian, it doesn't mean they will stop making mistakes or sinning. They might less, but they'll never stop; it's impossible. Every one of us makes mistakes, and Jesus died for every single one of us. He didn't die for only those who believe in Him, or just those who don't believe Him.

He died for us all, there is no one better than another, whether they believe in Christ or not—He shows no partiality; we all make mistakes.

Can you imagine having one literally perfect son and having to send Him to die on a cross for undeserving people who mock him?

God did this for us because He loves us so dearly, and He wanted a way for us to be in heaven with Him.

He had his Son die for our sins and gave us the promise that whoever believes in Him will have eternal life.

If you ask me, that is definitely the nicest gift anyone will and did ever do for us. It's amazing because God had his Son die for us so that we won't die of our sines if we choose to believe in him.

The selfless act Jesus performed is incredible, not only because He died on a cross for us but because He is mocked every day and judged constantly. But He still gave His life for the people committing these acts.

When you are being judged, or maybe someone questions your Christianity because you made a mistake, remember what I just told you about God sending His one and only perfect Son to die for us so we don't have to die from our sins.

He was nailed to the cross after being beaten so He can forgive us, show us His love, mercy, and grace as well as give us the opportunity and chance to be with Him in Heaven, forever. Remember who you are in Christ, and most importantly, remember what God thinks of you.

Let God judge you, not others. His forgiveness is the most important, as well as His judgment, which is just and impartial. Look to God during these hurtful times and remember when you make a mistake and someone judges you, they do not matter because they are not the one opening the gates to Heaven—God is.

Judgment can hurt, especially when you are a Christian and you are being mocked for it, but Jesus was mocked and is still mocked. He knows your pain and you will one day be greatly rewarded for your faithfulness.

John 3:17 says, "For God did not send his Son into the world to condemn the world, but to save the world through him."

Have courage and have hope, because the Lord isn't here to tell you that you are wrong and to judge you, but to save you ultimately. He desires to protect and teach you.

You will make mistakes, and the world will judge you and may even mock you, but the Lord forgives and strengthens you; He renews you.

You may think you have done the most awful things in this world, but there is hope for everyone, He proclaims.

Let's take this next step to uninvite the hurt we feel from being mocked and slandered. Uninvite the pain from being judged from the world.

Take the time to do it, because you have someone else here to give you peace and to give you comfort. You don't have time for these things to keep you from your purpose.

You don't have time for it, simple as that.

Be hopeful today, because the Almighty already told you can be saved from your sins when you choose to believe in Him and repent.

Day 50: Tattle Technique

When my siblings and I were younger, and we would get into trouble with our parents, we would tattletale and compare each other to make ourselves look better in hopes of not being punished. For example, if I got in trouble for talking back to my parents and they punished me or reprimanded me for it, I would start to mention how my brother or sister stayed out too late, or a time they talked back. I'm sure most—if not all—siblings do this to each other.

Essentially, I would speak upon their mistakes to distract them from what I did. This would happen in school, as well, when one child would get in trouble with a teacher and they would tattletale on the other children.

You will find that there are certain people who will point their finger at you for something you did and think they are better than you. In reality, we all sin and there is not one person God looks at and says is better or worse than us, because to Him, sin is sin. There is not one sin that is more okay than the other.

For Romans 3:10 says, "There is no one righteous, not even one;"

We should not judge each other for what we do—that is God's job. The Lord tells us in 1 John chapter 3 that when we hate someone, it's the same thing as committing murder.

Do you see where I am going with this? If you judge a murderer and say you are better than them and that God loves you more, it's not true at all. All sin is just as bad in God's eyes, He hates all sin. He doesn't pick out a few and say, "These would be okay" or "These few are not so bad; I'll be lenient." We all sin. I have seen and have heard many people say, "At least I don't do this" or "At least I am not a murderer." The Lord tells us that hating one another, destroying their life, slandering or "striking someone with your tongue", is just as bad as murder. Leave the judgment up to God because if you sin, you are a sinner like the person in jail or the person who was caught stealing.

We often try to point out other people's sins, like children do to each other as if we are using that technique with God. Don't try to point out someone else's sin while dealing with your own to make yourself more comfortable living with guilt. When I use tattling as a comparison to when we're a child, I use it in a sense of distracting the feelings of guilt you have when you're at fault by digging into someone else's weaknesses and faults.

Rather than pointing out what someone else has done, pray for them, and encourage them to defeat their temptations—be in fellowship to strengthen one another to be more like Christ.

We are all a team and we all fall short as we are all sinners.

Never feel bad about yourself and think you are less worthy than someone else, that you are less in God's eyes, or think that you are above someone because you haven't done what they have.

Remember, I can't stand that word "less." This is another reason why. People tell each other they're less in God's eyes when it's not true at all because He loves all of His children the same.

While unfortunately that can be the case here on earth with people in your life calling you less, or making you feel less, it is never the case with God. Be encouraged, and please encourage. Make that your motto.

Don't try to avoid your sins and feelings of guilt by pointing out that you haven't done what others have and try to make yourself feel better about it, because we all fall short and we all are sinners. He knows what you're doing. Don't try to use the tattletale tactic with God; He knows what you are avoiding. He also sees all things, he knows what other people have done and he knows what you do. When you try to make yourself feel better about your wrong doings by saying, "At least I don't do this" or while talking to God saying, "I did this, but I haven't done this" know that there are no compromises with Him and there are no sins that He feels "Okay" about. We're all sinners and we are all at fault. Don't use the tattle technique when you're being disciplined, He will deal with other people's sinful actions as He will deal with ours too. Instead of beating people down to make yourself feel better, help one another, defeat temptation together, and get right with God.

Romans 2:11 says, "For God does not show favoritism."

Uninvite these feelings of partiality as if you are less in God's eyes. Don't allow tattletales in your life, and don't allow yourself to do it either, for God is in charge of judging—not us. Be encouraged today because He does not count the sins you commit and compare it with others. He wants us to be helpful to each other and not point out the dirt, rather dig for the gold in each other. Allow encouragement to overtake your life, for two is better than one. A team in Christ is better than none.

(Bonus Day) Day 51: He Loves You, Not BECAUSE

You will always hear someone talk about why they love their wife or their husband, or their boyfriend or girlfriend. Further, you hear people say why they love their boss, or a certain food, even different products, too.

Most of the reasons are followed by the word "because," if you ever notice that. People say they love so and so because of certain reasons.

The word following is always "because," which means a reason is coming. You know when someone says they love your dog because he or she is so cute and cuddly, or because they are well-behaved and loving, or they love their boyfriend for such and such reasons.

It is often followed by a "because," because there is a reason.

Something I hear many people say is, "God loves me because I repent", or "God loves me because I tithe."

I even hear certain people say, "God loves me because I am a virgin."

This one is the most typical: "God loves me because I help people."

Well, God may appreciate that you do those things and serve Him this way, but that's not why He loves you. You don't have to be an excellent person for Him to love you.

Obviously, He wants you to live as the Word says and try to be like Him every day, but that is nowhere near why He loves you.

Also, if you feel sad today about that because maybe you're not a virgin or anywhere near close to one, maybe you don't repent as often as you should, or you don't tithe, don't feel like God doesn't love you. He does and He knows your heart.

Some people may judge you upon your actions or the story behind your life, but they don't know you fully as they were not the One who created you. God loves you regardless. There is no "because."

God commends His love for each and every one of us, and never said "because." The Lord proclaims it. He says we are enough, not that we are perfect and do great things. No, He loves us, and that is it. He commended it.

Look at Romans 5:8 which proclaims, "But God demonstrates his own love for us in this: While we were still sinners, Christ died for us."

God does not love you because of anything you do—He just loves you. The fact He died for us is amazing, but loving us while we are still sinners is a love that I cannot understand.

We mock Him, we disobey Him, and we turn our backs on Him, yet He still loves us unconditionally.

Thinking about it, I don't understand why we would want to disobey someone who died for us, protects us, blesses us, and so on. I know we are sinners, and we will sin, the Lord tells us that. We are incapable of being perfect, which stems from Adam and Eve's disobedience as well as being incapable of perfection, but we should strive to be the best we can be for Him.

Today, if you're feeling like you are not loved by God because you are not godly and don't act as other people you see in a church or somewhere else, know that He loves you. There is no "because." He just does. He commended it.

Uninvite the doubt you have or the shame you feel—you have Christ around you, in your heart forever, so you don't need uneasy feelings. You should feel loved.

Be joyful, for the Lord is on your side.

(Bonus Day) Day 52: Labor Pains

I am not a mom yet, but I do have a mom, a grandmother, and friends who are moms and the process of birth has been explained to me explicitly over and over again.

So for what I have been told, and of course I've never experienced this for myself, when you go through labor— the pain from it is like nothing you've ever felt before, but the main thing is, is that it's worth it.

Contractions are the indication that your child is coming. It's the time that he or she is ready to be with you; they are ready for the world. You go through these horrible, painful moments, and then maybe some not so bad parts, but overall, it's painful.

Once you and your baby are ready, you push so that your child is born. When you push, you're tired—not even tired. Exhausted is the word most people use.

You're in pain and you are ready for the victorious sweet baby you've waited months for. Finally, after the long journey, your beautiful creation is born.

The pain was worth it. You got your victory. After all those months of pregnancy and hours of labor, you delivered your precious angel that you waited so patiently (or not so patiently) for, you see face to face the purpose of your pain.

In life we also experience labor pains. We go through a long, long journey of discomfort and sometimes some comfortable times until our victory and our glory is delivered. Just like the process of birth, we have to go through these contractions and horribly painful labor pains in order to grow and deliver our victory.

We have to push through the hard parts and conquer, even when we're so exhausted we feel we can't do it anymore.

You have to go through a "pregnancy" season in your life in order to grow, mature, and be more confident in your relationship with Christ until victory comes. During this time you might have to go through some uncomfortable times like some women feel while pregnant.

Nothing in this life on earth will be easy, but it can be worth it if we put our faith in God and conquer the pain and get through the contractions. Once you are through these raw, natural, and explicitly cringing pains, your deliverance from evil is entirely and undoubtedly worth it.

You receive your miracle.

Psalm 34:4 proclaims, "I sought the LORD, and He answered me; he delivered me from all my fears."

The Lord will deliver you from all your fears, your pain, your anxieties, and worries.

Go through the labor pains that life brings you with the Lord and use His strength He gives you. Uninvite the feelings of exhaustion and thoughts like you can't do it. You have victory to see face to face. You don't have time to doubt yourself because it is delaying you from your purpose and keeping you from your victory.

You can get through this season of pain and hurt; your victory is coming, your miracle is waiting to be born. Trust in God and have hope always because your time

has come. Be patient for His timing is everything.

Congratulations:

After all the adversity you've been through—the heartache, the pain, the open wounds stinging, and the rawest sadness you ever faced—you are here, reading this book and persevering.

You're getting through it.

After all the moments you couldn't breathe and you wondered: *How and why can life go on after this? What will I do? How do I move past this, or what is the point?*

You are here and you are continuing. You're conquering.

So keep doing what you're doing right now: standing firm. Don't you move. You can survive this thing you are going through, and you will. Many people in your life may not know issues you may deal with day to day, and I may not know it either, but the Lord does and is waiting to be with you. He brought you hope, and it's your gift, so receive it. You made it this far and you have to keep going.

Reflect right now on what you have been through: the toughest waves, the difficult climbs, and swimming through the scariest seas, filled with constant doubt that life pegs straight to your heart.

Now, since you know and believe there is unwavering love, hope, and faith from Jesus, it gets much easier. So congratulations on getting through this journey, you didn't give up. You conquered. You're still here.

The Lord is seeing you through all of this and He is proud of you. You are His survivor. He is sovereign, remember that. He has supreme rule over your life so do not fear, there is no time for that! Especially when the devil attacks because the Lord's power is greater than his.

You may not see the power God has over your life, but that is because He is working behind the scenes. He is setting things up in your favor so diligently. All you have to do is be here, stand with Him, believe and obey. You have survived the storms, so don't you move!

As Psalm 107:29 says, "He stilled the storm to a whisper; the waves of the sea were hushed."

Look what the Lord has done in your life. You are here reading this book, surviving, and trying your best to get through this difficult journey you are in. You conquered the seas and you didn't give up. All those times you thought this was it and you couldn't do it anymore, God told you that you could, and now you're here. You are still here and you're getting closer.

Nehemiah 8:10 proclaims, Nehemiah said, "Go and enjoy choice food and sweet drinks, and send some to those who have nothing prepared. This day is holy to our Lord. Do not grieve, for the joy of the LORD is your strength."

You have strength from the Lord! It is directly from Him. Do you know how powerful that is? Have joy in this, for you are a survivor as you are still here, you haven't quit—you made progress. You are doing so much better than you think. Remember that when you try, it is the beginning of success and look at you now—you are trying. So be joyful today on the improvements you have

The Unfinished Puzzle   Ashley Alice White

made.

Congratulations, truly.

Arrival

When you are on a plane, traveling to your final destination, sometimes the plane goes against the wind.

It still gets to where it needs to go, but it has something to go against; it has to push through the wind to finally arrive. Some days there is a lot of turbulence throughout the journey, and then some days there is not.

Further, it can be easier some days to go against the wind and then some days quite difficult, but overall it is a challenge. When you are trying to get to your final destination, where God has called you to be, don't you think you will have to go against the wind too?

You will always have to face opposition; some days are harder than others, but you will always face it traveling to your destination, your purpose.

Be aware that you may face turbulence too in your time of travels, but it is always in God's hands. He will always see you through. You're never alone while facing the wind or dealing with turbulence.

When facing your opposition, you may feel alone and that there is no way out of the darkness. You might even feel like it's never ending, and you won't reach your destination, like you are in a storm that won't calm. I have felt this way many times, but most recently while dealing with a health condition.

My sickness, cancer, was the wind—even worse—it was a storm. I was trying to reach goals I set for myself, such as writing this book and many other things that were hard to push through.

I was flying, soaring even, and felt the turbulence hit hard.

As I was dealing with this and naturally became overwhelmingly discouraged, I was reminded of **Deuteronomy 31:8 which says, "The Lord himself goes before you and will be with you; He will never leave you nor forsake you. Do not be afraid; do not be discouraged."**

Let that sink in a bit. I repeated it a few times, as I needed to. You should too. I was alone in doctor's office waiting for my test results and had to repeat to myself that the Lord is already here. He said Himself He is before us.

There was another time as well, perhaps an even scarier time where I had to repeat out loud that the Lord is before me. I woke up from surgery in excruciating pain. For about an hour there was nothing that could resolve it, all I held onto was the hope I had from God where I repeated over and over again that He is before me. When I was left with what it seemed like in the moment nothing, I had God to hold onto.

He is there. He won't leave and He will walk me through. Surely this didn't make my pain disappear right then and there, but it is in fact the only and very thing that pulled me through the rest of that day. I held onto the hope I had in our Savior watching over me and standing before me.

He's there; He knows what it takes to get you there. He has the solution already whether you can see it or not.

I had to instill this in my mind, that whatever I am dealing with, He is already there before me, waiting. We should never worry.

We should be anxious about nothing, because the Lord is already there.

You know certain times when you are doing something scary and you don't want to be the first one to do whatever you are doing?

Although, once your friend or family member goes first, you feel so much better because you see they already made it and are okay.

When I am dealing with an issue, that's how I feel. I feel at peace because I know God's already there. He's waiting for me. He went first, and He will not let me drown.

Don't be discouraged while facing opposition. Keep pushing through, especially because the Lord is already at your destination and He is cheering you on.

The turbulence may feel tough—unbearable even—but God does not give you anything you cannot handle.

He's waiting for you at your final destination, which gives us hope, because He promises to never leave.

Ladies and gentleman, you have arrived at your final destination: Hope.

For safety purposes, do not let the opposition you face discourage you, and do not let the turbulence interrupt your purpose and destination the Lord prepared for you.

I thank you dearly and forever for choosing to take your journey with me in this book, *The Unfinished Puzzle*.

Please fly with me again, and I hope you enjoyed your ride.

One more thing before you go. Don't forget to grab a complimentary bag that is filled with hope, peace, and love from

The Unfinished Puzzle   Ashley Alice White

the Captain, our Lord and Savior, Jesus Christ.

Aloha

The Unfinished Puzzle Checklist of Important Points

Ashley Alice White

Download the FREE printable Unfinished Puzzle Checklist that goes along with the devotional or can be used on its own-- PLUS a free short story!

AT WWW.ASHLEYAWHITEAUTHOR.COM

✓ Think of your life as an unfinished puzzle where you only see certain pieces. Some are scattered, and some don't fit in certain areas. It's frustrating to us because we can't see the whole picture yet. Sometimes we just see a glimpse, and other times it looks like nothing at all.

✓ Trust God with your puzzle. He sees the whole picture and knows where everything goes. After all, He created it.

✓ Trust in God. Know He sees the whole picture, and He will not waste your pain.

✓ So, my advice is to surrender your puzzle. When you stop forcing things to happen or fit together, like we sometimes do with puzzles when we can't figure them out, you can give it up to God. Surrender. God's plans He made for you before you were born will unfold, and you will come to see they are far beyond what you have ever dreamed.

✓ However, if we do not have it from God, it won't be the real thing.

✓ We cannot let fear interrupt our hopes and prayers because the Creator of the universe is a lot bigger than fear. Do not allow anymore interruptions.

✓ God is in control at all times. He calms all storms.

✓ Don't be cliché with God. He created you and he knows you. He designed your heart. Think of the riskiest idea, feeling, or thing you hope for, and pray hard. Ask him for it.

✓ When you have hope in God, you cannot lose, and you cannot drown. Be hopeful that the Lord is with you during these times where He can use your troubles for good.

✓ Get to know the rock bottom you hit and the emotions that

accompany it. Enjoy a cup of coffee with it! Stay a while.

✓ As Psalm 119:50 says, "My comfort in my suffering is this: Your promise preserves my life."

✓ Even when you hit rock bottom, you have many promises from God, and you'll still get out of the water. The Lord knows exactly how much you can handle, and He knows why you've hit the floor. Feel comforted, today, because the Lord goes with you and he will comfort you when you're at your lowest.

✓ Greet rock bottom. Welcome it. Address it with the promises from God and hang in there.

✓ "God created each day, and each day is a new day God can create a new opportunity."

✓ Although you and I may not be experiencing a natural disaster at this very moment where our house or neighborhood has been wiped out, I am sure there are aspects in your life that have been wiped out and feel like a disaster where you have to start all over again.

✓ With anything that is happening in your life right now or has happened, there is hope.

✓ Each day is a new opportunity for a new creation. Many of the words throughout the Bible, especially in the very beginning, say "God created."

✓ Pray to God and ask Him for a new creation. Something might be broken in your life, but the Lord can create something from that.

✓ Genesis 1:1 says, "In the beginning God created the heavens and the earth."

✓ He created then, He creates now, and He will create.

✓ When thinking of problems you have, don't think that you have a big problem. Instead know and believe you have a big God. He is bigger than anything you have to face.

✓ Deuteronomy 20:4 says, "For the Lord your God is the one who goes with you to fight for you against your enemies to give you victory."

✓ God doesn't leave you, even in the scariest situations where you feel He abandoned you, He pulls through.

✓ The Lord tells us, "You've got a friend in me."

✓ John 15:13 says, "Greater love has no one than this: to lay down one's life for one's friends."

✓ Think of God as your best friend who died for you, because he did as well as go through pain, anguish and discomfort before the cross just for us. Which of your friends would lay down their life for you?

✓ Imagine no pain at all, on this earth. Would we ever learn, or we would just stay the same and become dull and possibly ignorant?

✓ The Lord can identify with our pain, always.

✓ When you are in pain, with open wounds, wondering why you feel this way and how to stop it, know that the Lord will not waste your pain.

✓ Lean on God not only through times of pain and adversity, but through happy times and blessed times.

✓ When you don't see the purpose yet, you will learn and

strengthen your faith in the meantime.

✓ Romans 8:18 "I consider that our present sufferings are not worth comparing with the glory that will be revealed in us."

✓ You may be in a lot of pain now, but it will not be compared to the joy the Lord will bring you.

✓ The Lord knows your true heart, your true intentions, and the true honest work you do, and for that you will be rewarded one day with him. Do not be discouraged today if you feel you are not rewarded and a lot of what you do goes unnoticed.

✓ For Colossians 3:23-24 says, "Whatever you do, work at it with all your heart, as working for the Lord, not for human masters, since you know that you will receive an inheritance from the Lord as a reward. It is the Lord Christ you are serving."

✓ It's natural to desire to do well. The thing you need to be careful of is idolizing rewards from human masters.

✓ These things we may use to make us feel better, just like bandages, will not last forever. They are temporary fixes. They cover the injury up but do not heal them. These bandages, such as alcohol, sex, drugs, shopping, or overeating will not help with the root of your problem. It won't heal your pain. It just temporarily numbs it.

✓ Remember Psalm 147:3, which says, "He heals the broken hearted and binds up their wounds."

✓ Always remember, He heals.

✓ Let God control where you go, knowing that He has the reins. Obey Him when he tells you to stop or to keep going. Do not try to take your own path when you are blind to where you're going. You don't have the reins—God does. He is the only one with them, so don't try to take them and be in control.

✓ Psalm 25:4-5 says, "Make me know your ways, LORD, teach me your paths. Guide me in your truth and teach me, for you are God my Savior, and my hope is in you all day long".

✓ Take today to think on areas in your life where you need to let go of the reins you stole from Him. Let God take the reins.

✓ We cannot divorce God when bad times come. That would be like saying, "When I am happy and see You do works in my life, I will praise You, but if something bad happens and I don't understand it, I'm gone."

✓ Say, "I do" and mean it. Take action on it. Praise Him always, even more in the bad times, for that's when you are learning and strengthening your faith. He knows what He is doing, so have faith even when you don't understand.

✓ Psalm 34:1-3 says it perfectly, "I will extol the Lord at all times; his praise will always be on my lips. I will glorify in the LORD; let the afflicted hear and rejoice. Glorify the LORD with me; let us exalt his name together."

✓ Wait for the dessert that is coming, and hold your fork; hold it high. Grab a hold of it and don't let go.

✓ Job 11:18-19 says, "You will be secure, because there is hope; you will look about you and take your rest in safety. You will lie down, with no one to make you afraid, and many will court your favor."

✓ Hold your fork, and hold it high! For the Lord is waiting to give you what you are unable to possibly imagine. There will always be dessert worth waiting for.

✓ If you read God's word every day, even just a little bit each day, you will tone your mind.

✓ You will build a great foundation in Christ by learning more about Him. You will know Him much more than before. Listen to what the Bible is saying. Really listen.

✓ If you read half of the Bible all in one sitting then not read again until another month or two, your foundation and knowledge won't last long.

✓ Mathew 7:24-27 says, "Therefore everyone who hears these words of mine and puts them into practice is like a wise man who built his house on rock. The rain came down, the streams rose, and the winds blew and beat against that house; yet it did not fall, because it had its foundation on the rock. But everyone who hears these words of mine and does not put them into practice is like a foolish man who built his house on sand. The rain came down, the streams rose, and the winds blew and beat against that house, and it fell with a great crash."

✓ Which issues in your life are in urgent need of a solution? Start making these problems at the top of your list. Mark them as an urgent need.

✓ As Psalm 50:15 says, "And call on me in the day of trouble; I will deliver you, and you will honor me."

✓ As we have troubles that need immediate attention, we should call on the Lord daily. He will help us, but we need to make sure we treat them as urgent needs and not ignore them. Do not let your problems that need urgent attention linger so they hinder you from the potential the Lord has for you.

✓ As I was sitting in front of the Tomb of the Unknown Soldier waiting to watch the switch of the guards, I started to think about different things like how we as individuals are each at war every day—a spiritual war, that is.

✓ Every day the enemy is attacking our minds, our hearts, and our souls. The enemy wants to destroy our conscience and keep us from getting closer to God.

✓ 2nd Timothy 2:3 says, "Join me in suffering, like a good soldier of Christ Jesus."

✓ We are in spiritual warfare every day and we are the soldiers of Christ. Every day it is essential for you to wake up and believe you will win the fight the devil put against you.

✓ One powerful verse I hope you remember wherever you go, is Joshua 1:9: "Have I not commanded you? Be strong and courageous. Do not be afraid; do not be discouraged, for the Lord your God is with you wherever you go."

✓ Bring out the fighter in you and conquer the battles the enemy puts in your mind and heart. You can do it, you have the Lord on your side.

✓ Our eternal home is permanent. We must choose wisely, now, right this second, because we are placed in our home forever when the time comes.

✓ Once we are in His home, we are there forever. We will never move.

✓ He set aside a special place for us, so we can be with Him forever. Doesn't that make you smile?

✓ For John 3:16 says, "For God so loved the world that he gave his one and only Son, for whoever believes in Him shall not perish but have eternal life."

✓ .John 14:2-4 says, "My Father's house has many rooms; if that were not so, would I have told you that I am going there to prepare a place for you? And if I go and prepare a place for you, I will come back and take you to be with me that you also may be where I am. You know the way to the place where I am going."

✓ God created many different languages that people speak, and sometimes it's extremely frustrating to not be able to comprehend what others are saying, but other times it's so beautiful because you can exchange what you want to say through actions and emotions.

✓ Even if we can't understand each other through speaking, the love Jesus gives us can be shown through one another even when words are not always exchanged. And sometimes these actions truly are louder than words.

✓ Listen to what Zephaniah 3:9 says: "Then I will purify the lips of the peoples, that all of them may call on the name of the LORD and serve him shoulder to shoulder."

✓ We think we are doing well by praying to God, asking and seeking. But are we actually seeking? Seeking is looking for God's perfect plan and asking Him for that, not the ungodly things we want because those certainly won't come from the Lord.

✓ We need to make sure we really understand how God works, not only in the way of how He makes things happen or how He creates, but in terms of our relationship with Him. He knows us better than we know ourselves.

✓ You may ask, and He may say no, but He doesn't say no without a reason behind it. When He says no, we fail to understand that there's a reason, such as God having something far more significant in store.

✓ He didn't fail me, I just confused what I thought was failure with His plan.

✓ Do not confuse His plan and His protection with Him failing you.

✓ John 8:32 says, "Then you will know the truth, and the truth will set you free."

✓ While inevitably going through the dark, horrid tunnels we have to go through in some parts of our lives, we can strive every day to see the light which comes from the Lord. If you spot the smallest glimpse of light in your life, strive to get there.

✓ God gives us a future, so we don't have to dwell in our past! He secures our future and provides a way out of our past. Every day we need to look for the light, to find our destination that God set out for us.

✓ "The LORD is my light and my salvation—whom shall I fear? The LORD is the stronghold of my life—of whom shall I be afraid?" -Psalm 27:1

✓ Just like needing water in order to live, we need God's Word to truly live.

✓ To live free and not be in the bondage of our sins, we have to hydrate ourselves in the Word of God to constantly know Him, be encouraged, and live according to His Word.

✓ John 7:38 says, "Whoever believes in me, as scripture has said, rivers of living water will flow from within them."

✓ Think of problems as prerequisites for miracles. This means you have to have a problem before you have a miracle. How could we have miracles if there are no problems in need of a miracle?

✓ You might not understand the problem that you have now, but there will be a miracle in the end. The problem has to happen in order for the miracle to come—a problem or trial is the prerequisite.

✓ If a problem comes our way, and we have God in our hearts, you know He has a miracle heading your way, because He never wastes pain! Think positively about your problems because a miracle is coming your way. When I say "miracle," I am not just talking about supernatural things happening. You may not know what your miracle is or know that it happened, but know now that the Lord has a plan for you and will not waste your pain.

✓ As Exodus 15: 26 says, He said, "If you listen carefully to the LORD your God and do what is right in his eyes, if you pay attention to his commands and keep all his decrees, I will not bring on you any of the diseases I brought on the Egyptians, for I am the LORD, who heals you."

✓ Do you treat God like company? Do you try to clean up everything that seems "messy" and unclean before letting God in?

✓ Why are you trying to pretend there are no messes in your life when He already sees them? Sometimes people feel like they are too messy or not good enough, maybe even have too much baggage to be with God, but that is not true because He already sees everything. He knows everything about us; we are not too messy for Him.

✓ He wants to clean you, so you don't need to. Let Him see the mess.

✓ John 10:14 "I am the good shepherd; I know my sheep and my sheep know me."

✓ Invite God into your real life and your messy, coffee-spilling, dirty-floored, messy-laundry home.

✓ Isaiah 43:2 says, "When you pass through the waters, I will be with you; and when you pass through the rivers, they will not sweep over you. When you walk through the fire, you will not be burned; the flames will not set you ablaze."

✓ I'll tell you now, trusting in God is easy and hard at the same time. A lot of you probably know that. When you have faith in the Lord and know that He will always come through, it is so much easier to trust in Him. Always associate the word trust with faith when it comes to God.

✓ You will never be hurt by God, and if you think you are, it's because what you want doesn't align with what He has planned for you.

✓ A title does not define you, your hard work does even when you do not have a title to match it.

✓ I'm not proud of this, but my mindset had been that once I achieve this or get that I'll be happy, and once I obtain a new success or save this much money I'll settle down and be satisfied. However, I've learned it doesn't stop there, because once I obtain all those things, there is something else that comes along as well as someone else who will do what I did, but better.

✓ I learned the hard way that it doesn't satisfy you, and I was seduced by the temporary happiness it brings.

✓ Don't be seduced by success.

✓ Sure, it's great to be successful and want to better yourself every day, which you absolutely should, but be careful with idolizing the success you obtain and the feeling of wanting to chase it more. It brings you down a dark road.

✓ Mathew 6:21 tells us, "For where your treasure is, there your heart will be also."

✓ This is telling us that what you admire and what makes you happy (your treasure) there your heart will be.

✓ Do not let that treasure be success, let it be God.

✓ Exodus 20:3 "You shall have no other God's before me."

✓ Do not get discouraged. Everything He has planned for you is in the works of the Most High God we serve. He is not forgetting you. It is just in His time, not yours.

✓ John 5:17 says, "Jesus said to them, 'My Father is always at his work, to this very day, and I, too, am working.'"

✓ Never doubt the significance of your trials, because they are what lead you to where God wants you to be.

✓ Have hope today because the Lord is working all day and all night on the plan He has for your life. He never gives up on you and will always see you through, even through delays.

✓ When you are climbing to your destination in life for the purpose God created you for, you should make sure the slack is a good amount, but the support is focused and strong. You need a firm supporter. Make sure the person supporting you knows the right amount that you need, otherwise they are not a good fit.

✓ Ecclesiastes 4:9-12 says, "Two are better than one, because they have a good return for their labor: If either of them falls down, one can help the other up. But pity anyone who falls and has no one to help them up. Also, if two lie down together, they will keep warm. But how can one keep warm alone? Though one may be overpowered, two can defend themselves. A cord of three strands is not quickly broken."

✓ Psalm 37:23 says, "The LORD makes firm the steps of the one who delights in him."

✓ As our steps are ordered by the Lord, we must make sure we follow each and every step He has for us because we know His way is perfect.

✓ Do not question Him or doubt Him. That just insults our precious father. Have faith and trust that the Lord does not and will not forget you.

✓ Psalm 94:14 proclaims, "For the Lord will not reject his people; He will never forsake His inheritance."

✓ If you feel abandoned, remember that it is impossible for God to leave you, therefore you will never be abandoned. When you feel like He left you lonesome with your troubles, my precious advice is to calm down and don't move. Be still. He's there.

✓ Don't hang by a thread. The Lord says to call upon Him during times of trouble and to be anxious about nothing. We can rehearse this walk of life, and it doesn't have to be scary and wobbly. We can be strong and stand firm in the faith we have in God to help us through, so we can gloriously stride confidently along the tight rope we associate with life.

✓ 1 Corinthians 16:13 tells us, "Be on your guard; stand firm in the faith; be courageous; be strong."

✓ Are we living for this world and wanting to serve it and make them happy? Or, are we living for God and looking for His loving words of "well done"?

✓ Live to hear the Lord tell you "well done" not the rest of the world. They don't have a plan for you like He does.

✓ As Mathew 25:23 says, "His master replied, 'Well done, good and faithful servant! You have been faithful with a few things; I will put you in charge of many things. Come and share your master's happiness!'"

✓ Don't live life trying to please the world with what they want and want to hear. They can't give you true happiness, peace, or eternal life—only God can.

✓ Our timing is not always right because we tend to get impatient and rush, or we pick the wrong time for a lot of things because we don't know everything like the Lord does. God's timing is always perfect, and we need to rely on that, not our own understanding.

✓ As Ecclesiastes 8:6 proclaims, "For there is a proper time and procedure for every matter, though a person may be weighed down by misery."

✓ We are so blessed to have a God that never backs out. We never have to have doubt or fear during these trust falls in our life because He doesn't hesitate.

✓ For Psalm 31:14 says, "But I trust in you, Lord; I say, 'You are my God.'"

✓ Keep repeating this to yourself.: He is your God. He is behind you at all times, ready for a trust fall while we are in this world where things can go wrong.

✓ God knows us better than we know ourselves, always and He is constantly watching out for us. You were created excellently and on purpose by the Creator of the universe, so of course He knows your true heart's desires.

✓ Romans 8:27-28 explains, "And he who searches our hearts knows the mind of the Spirit, because the Spirit intercedes for God's people in accordance with the will of God. And we know that in all things God works for the good of those who love him, who have been called according to his purpose."

✓ If He says no, it's for a reason because He has our best interest. He's not doing it randomly or to be mean.

✓ Have peace in knowing the Lord sees your life as a whole picture. He dipped his brushes in glory and painted your victory.

✓ What/who are the mosquitoes in your life biting you and bringing you closer to your weaknesses? Maybe you would find God in being the bug spray in your life that protects you from these opportunities (except God works for everyone and bug spray may not).

✓ Don't forget to use it and protect yourself. If you do get bit, it's crucial to resist and put on the itch cream, which you may compare to the word of God.

✓ Read the word and really study it. Know it in your heart, for when your temptations come around—which they will because remember we can never avoid them—know what the Lord says.

✓ Remove all opportunities in your life that push you away from

God and resist the urges the world gives you that display themselves as nothing but happiness, but are actually tricks from the devil. You can do this, and once you do, it becomes easier. You'll feel amazing peace and joy from the Lord and you'll feel his true love that will sustain you.

✓ Trust in the strength that the Lord provides you. Remove and resist temptations.

✓ We can make plans all we want, but we must be prepared that if they are not from God, they may change whether we like it or not. It's not in our control, and it never will be.

✓ One of my favorite things to say is, "We make plans and God laughs."

✓ Our plans don't last, but God's do.

✓ It's important to always ask God for His will and for Him to bring us in His direction, because His plans are the best while ours often fail.

✓ Proverbs 16:1 says, "To humans belong the plans of the heart, but from the Lord comes the proper answer of the tongues."

✓ Jeremiah 1:5 "Before I formed you in the womb I knew you, before you were born I set you apart; I appointed you as a prophet to the nations."

✓ If we trust in Him and put all our worries and problems such as pain, doubt, guilt, and grief on Him, this homemade remedy gives us peace.

✓ The God of this universe gave His One and only Son to die for us, so the least we could do is trust in Him and use this homemade remedy from Him.

✓ John 14:27 tells us we can have peace. We are told, "Peace I leave with you; my peace I give you. I do not give to you as the world gives. Do not let your hearts be troubled and do not be afraid."

✓ What would we do without God as our remarkable life GPS? We sure don't know where we are going, and there are no certain maps to tell us our next step, which a lot of the time is terrifying. In life, we are lost without God, going in the wrong direction, not knowing where the next turn is, running stop signs and obvious red lights.

✓ Think of God as your GPS in life. He knows where to bring you. He knows your next turn, the next stop sign, and the next detour, so follow his way.

✓ Trust Him because He created the road and all the turns and road signs involved. You won't get lost if you believe, trust, and obey God.

✓ Psalm 25:10 says, "All the ways of the Lord are loving and faithful toward those who keep the demands of his covenant."

✓ Have hope in the fact that God will give you strength and always tell you when you need to stop, take a left, take a right or go straight.

✓ In life, if we do not lean with God when He leans, and we are not in sync during our ride with Him, we will fall, taking a hard tumble.

✓ Psalm 37:24, "Though he stumble, he will not fall, for the LORD upholds him with his hand."

✓ When you go on this ride with God, make sure you're in sync with him and lean when He takes a turn. You don't want to fall, but you don't have to be scared either. Don't fear, for He can see the entire road ahead when you cannot. The Lord has you in complete care.

✓ With God, we are always safe, even in the waves of adversity, misfortunes and tribulations that crash in on us.

✓ God is bigger than all of your problems. Be patient and you will see, He will pull you out of the water.

✓ As Isaiah 41:10 proclaims, "So do not fear, for I am with you; do not be dismayed, for I am your God. I will strengthen you and help you; I will uphold you with my righteous right hand."

✓ John 10:10 says, "The thief comes only to steal and kill and destroy; I have come that they may have life, and have it to the full."

✓ Do not let anyone steal your joy the Lord has blessed you with. The Lord intended it for you, only.

✓ I know you won't feel like looking on the bright side when bad things happen, which is why we need to have a good relationship with God because He is the bright side.

✓ The Lord decides and says, "No, this is not for you, I have something better, I have something else."

✓ Rejoice in the fact that God is picking you out, specifically, to do something else, to be with someone else. He has a perfect plan set out for you. You are not less than anything or anyone.

✓ Start each morning by proclaiming that, because it's true. There is no single person on this earth that you are less than. We are only less than the Almighty Father, who tells us we are enough, always.

✓ The word "less" should never enter your mind when you're thinking of yourself. You are less than no one, but please be careful with knowing that because you are also not higher than anyone.

✓ You most likely don't understand what you are going through and why, but the Lord does and He has a divine plan awaiting.

✓ There is no such thing as all closed doors. There is always going to be another door opened with God. You are good enough, and you have hope to a better future.

✓ When someone tells you no, understand that God is about to tell you yes to something greater.

✓ 2 Corinthians 3:5 says, "Not that we are competent in ourselves to claim anything for ourselves, but our competence comes from God."

✓ My forever friend is always there. He never leaves me, and He never leaves you.

✓ This makes me feel so much better during times of fear and doubt. I know the Lord felt heartache first, and I know that He understands and will always be with me.

✓ As Jesus not only tells us that not only are we more than enough, he tells us to put our pain on Him. Do you see how much He loves us? He died not only for our sins, but so we can lean on Him during our times of heartache and suffering.

✓ However, there is someone who does that every day, all day, and all night—no matter what the damage is. He does it with love, grace, mercy, and compassion. God promises to forgive us of our sins when we repentant, always.

✓ It doesn't matter how sad we make him with our disobedience,

He will always and forever forgive us when we ask from our hearts and turn from that sin.

✓ Without doing this, we break the fellowship we had with Him.

✓ This doesn't mean we can keep doing what we do that brings God great displeasure over and over again just because He forgives. If we don't confess before Him and truly repent, asking for strength with our weaknesses, then true blessings from Him will not come your way. You separate yourself from God when you refuse to confess and turn from your sin.

✓ Forgive the unforgiven people in your heart. Make some room for peace, love, joy, and especially, the Lord.

✓ As Colossians 3:13 says, "Bear with each other and forgive one another if any of you has a grievance against someone. Forgive as the Lord forgave you."

✓ Let go of those dark grudges. Don't let them cling to you—uninvite them.

✓ Forgive as the Lord forgave you and repent before Him. Bow down to the Lord who died for you. He's here to forgive you and bring salvation.

✓ I learned fully that the material things you want to chase won't make you rich or happy. Only satisfying yourself in the Lord is when you're richest of all, after all he always provides.

✓ Material things will not get you inside the golden gates with the Lord.

✓ When someone makes you feel unworthy and not important, when you are told you are not good enough and that you are not number one, remember that getting into heaven won't be chosen by who has the most money, or who has the most successes. So remember this verse.

- ✓ Mathew 20:16 says, "So the last will be first, and the first will be last."

- ✓ Luke 3:11 says, John answered "Anyone who has two shirts should share with the one who has none, and anyone who has food should do the same."

- ✓ Have peace in knowing that God will not waste your pain. He has a wonderful purpose for it, and you will see soon that it is used for good.

- ✓ Psalm 34:18 says, "The Lord is close to the brokenhearted and saves those who are crushed in spirit."

- ✓ During your times of pain and hurt—and especially confusion—on where the Lord is bringing you in your life, know that He will follow through. You may feel like you're sinking in the sand, but God won't let you, because He fully knows what you are capable of.

- ✓ 1 Corinthians 13:12 says, "For Now we see only a reflection as in a mirror; then we shall see face to face. Now I know in part; then I shall know fully, even as I am fully known."

- ✓ You're in temporary pain until victory is shown.

- ✓ We should move with God and never look back, only better our future and keep going. Like my soccer coach once told me, it only slows us down, so don't look back.

- ✓ You are new, so start new, and live new. Don't look back and slow yourself down.

- ✓ Genesis 19:26 says, "But Lot's wife looked back, and she became a pillar of salt."

✓ If you look back, that just sticks you in your past, and you won't be able to move forward if you keep looking there. When God forgives you, you need to also forgive yourself and move on. You can't go into your future when you're always looking back and not turning away.

✓ We as Christians are judged easily, and we're easy targets. I learned this the hard way. A lot of people judge us harder because they think we can't mess up or that we proclaim we don't.

✓ We will mess up. We are human. We all mess up and we make mistakes—daily, in fact.

✓ We are not God. None of us are, but we should try our best every day to show an example of Him and His love He always sheds on us unconditionally.

✓ The untold truth is if you mess up, and sometimes if you are a Christian and mess up, you will be judged harder because of the misconception people think you have to be or proclaim to be. You may even be slandered the way I was when I was abroad, hopefully not.

✓ Judgment can hurt, especially when you are a Christian and you are being mocked for it, but Jesus was mocked and is still mocked. He knows your pain and you will one day be greatly rewarded for your faithfulness.

✓ John 3:17 says, "For God did not send his Son into the world to condemn the world, but to save the world through him."

✓ Have courage and have hope, because the Lord isn't here to tell you that you are wrong and to judge you, but to save you ultimately. He desires to protect and teach you.

✓ You will make mistakes, and the world will judge you and may even mock you, but the Lord forgives and strengthens you; He renews you.

✓ For Romans 3:10 says, "There is no one righteous, not even one;"

✓ While unfortunately that can be the case here on earth with people in your life calling you less, or making you feel less, it is never the case with God. Be encouraged, and please encourage. Make that your motto.

✓ Don't try to avoid your sins and feelings of guilt by pointing out that you haven't done what others have and try to make yourself feel better about it, because we all fall short and we all are sinners. He knows what you're doing. Don't tattletale to God; He shows no favor.

✓ Romans 2:11 says, "For God does not show favoritism."

✓ God does not love you because of anything you do—He just loves you. The fact He died for us is amazing, but loving us while we are still sinners is a love that I cannot understand.

✓ We mock Him, we disobey Him, and we turn our backs on Him, yet He still loves us unconditionally.

✓ Psalm 34:4 proclaims, "I sought the LORD, and He answered me; he delivered me from all my fears."

✓ You can get through this season of pain and hurt; your victory is coming, your miracle is waiting to be born. Trust in God and have hope always because your time has come. Be patient for His timing is everything.

✓ As Psalm 107:29 says, "He stilled the storm to a whisper; the waves of the sea were hushed."

✓ Look what the Lord has done in your life. You are here reading this book, surviving, and trying your best to get through this difficult journey you are in. You conquered the seas and you didn't give up. All those times you thought this was it and you couldn't do it anymore, God told you that you could, and now you're here. You are still here and you're getting closer.

✓ Nehemiah 8:10 proclaims, Nehemiah said, "Go and enjoy choice food and sweet drinks, and send some to those who have nothing prepared. This day is holy to our Lord. Do not grieve, for the joy of the LORD is your strength."

✓ Deuteronomy 31:8 says, "The Lord himself goes before you and will be with you; He will never leave you nor forsake you. Do not be afraid; do not be discouraged."

To download the FREE printable version of this checklist, visit

www.AshleyAWhiteAuthor. com

-Ashley Alice White

25000537R00114

Made in the USA
Columbia, SC
01 September 2018